I0488895

Calmdalas

Adult Coloring Book

Over 50 Relaxing Mandalas to Color
One image per page

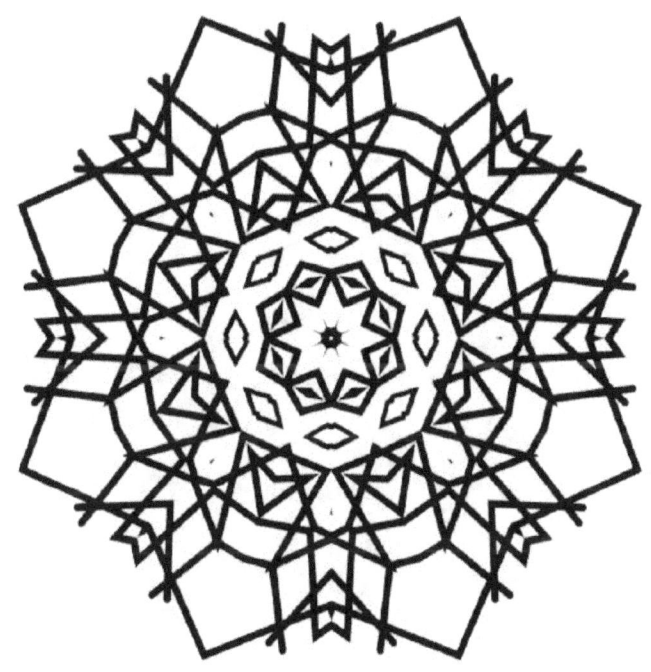

Sign up for our email list at www.calmdalas.com

Get notified about new books and get 10 **FREE** Calmdalas!

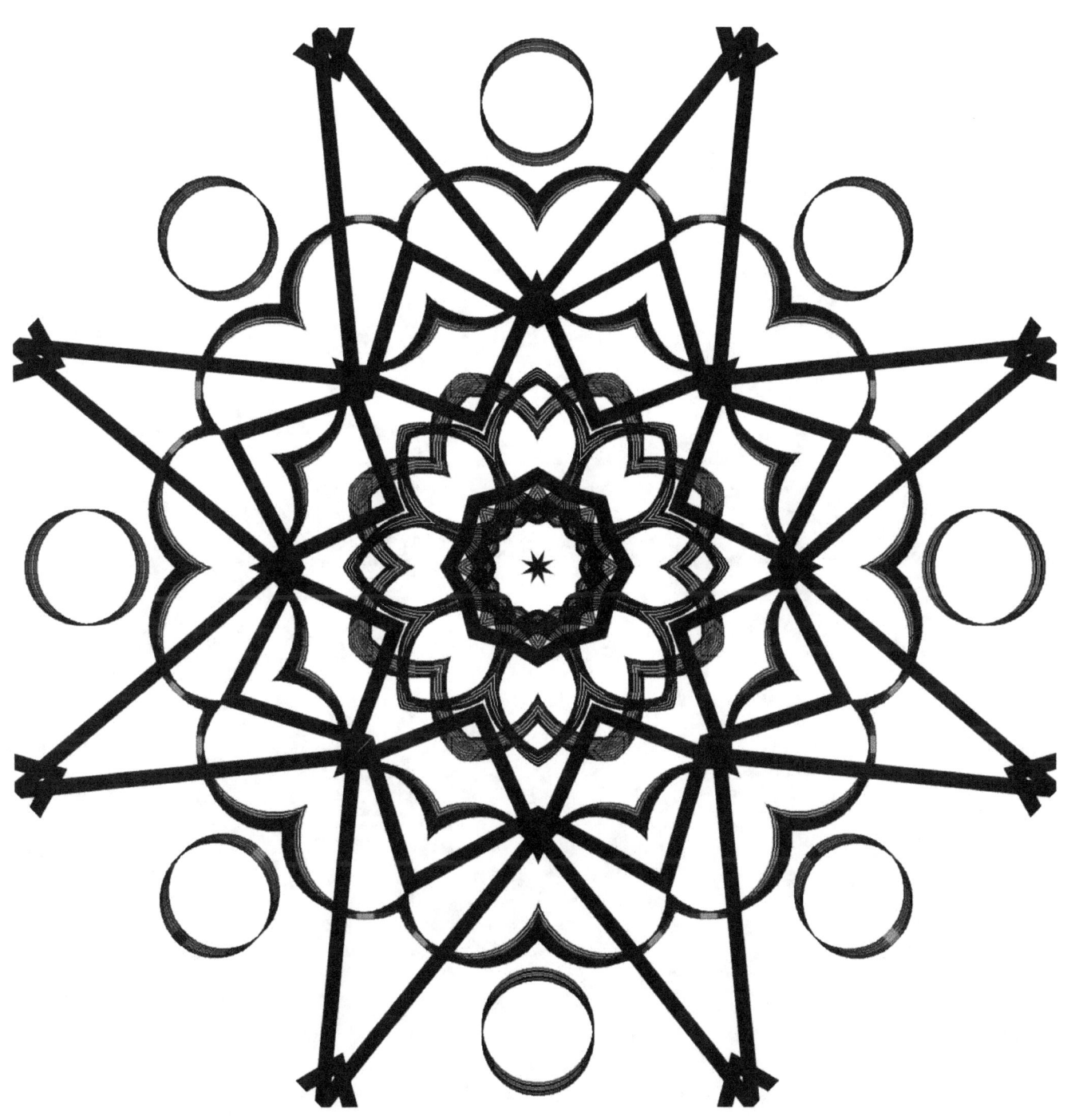

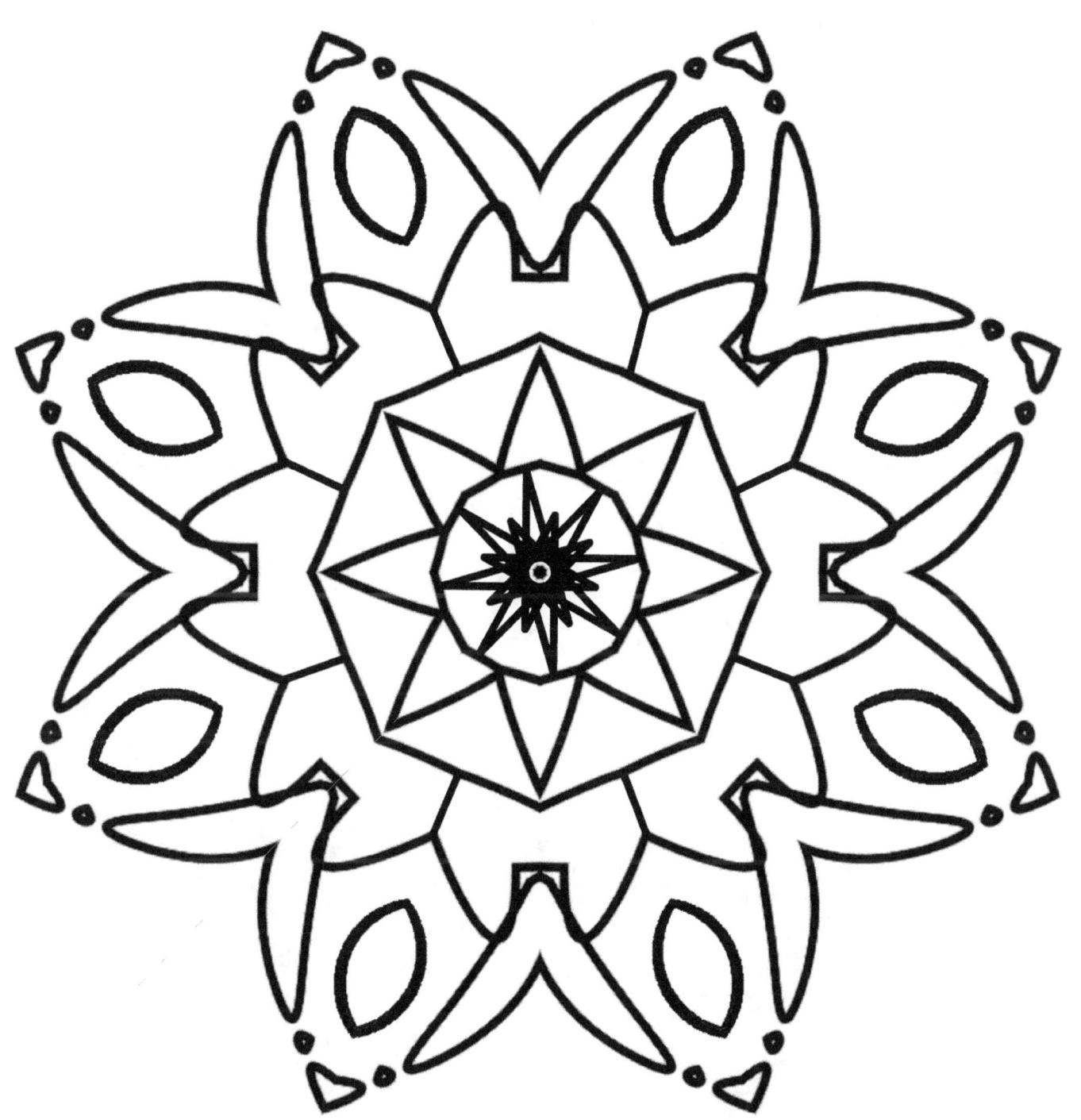

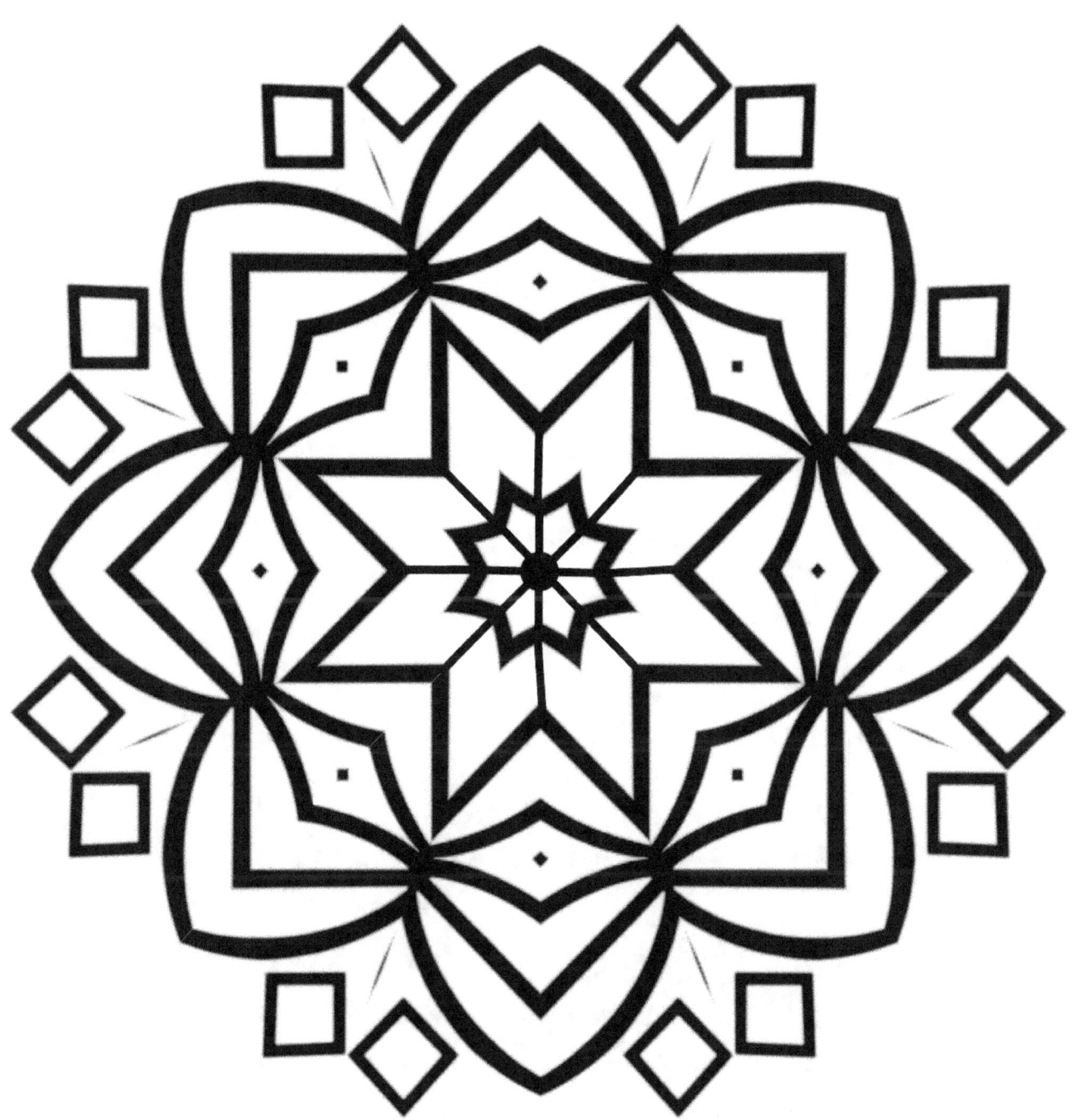

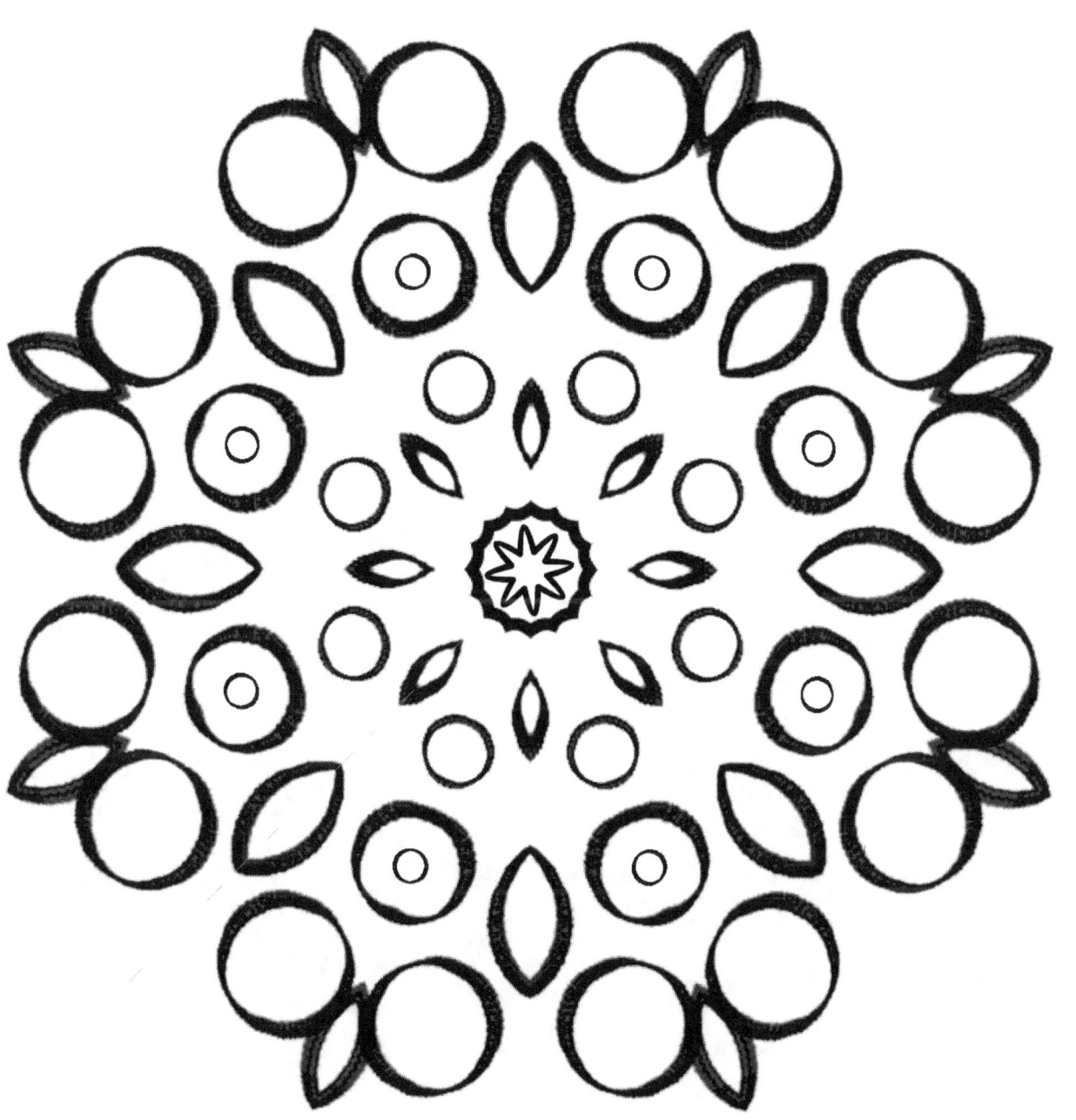

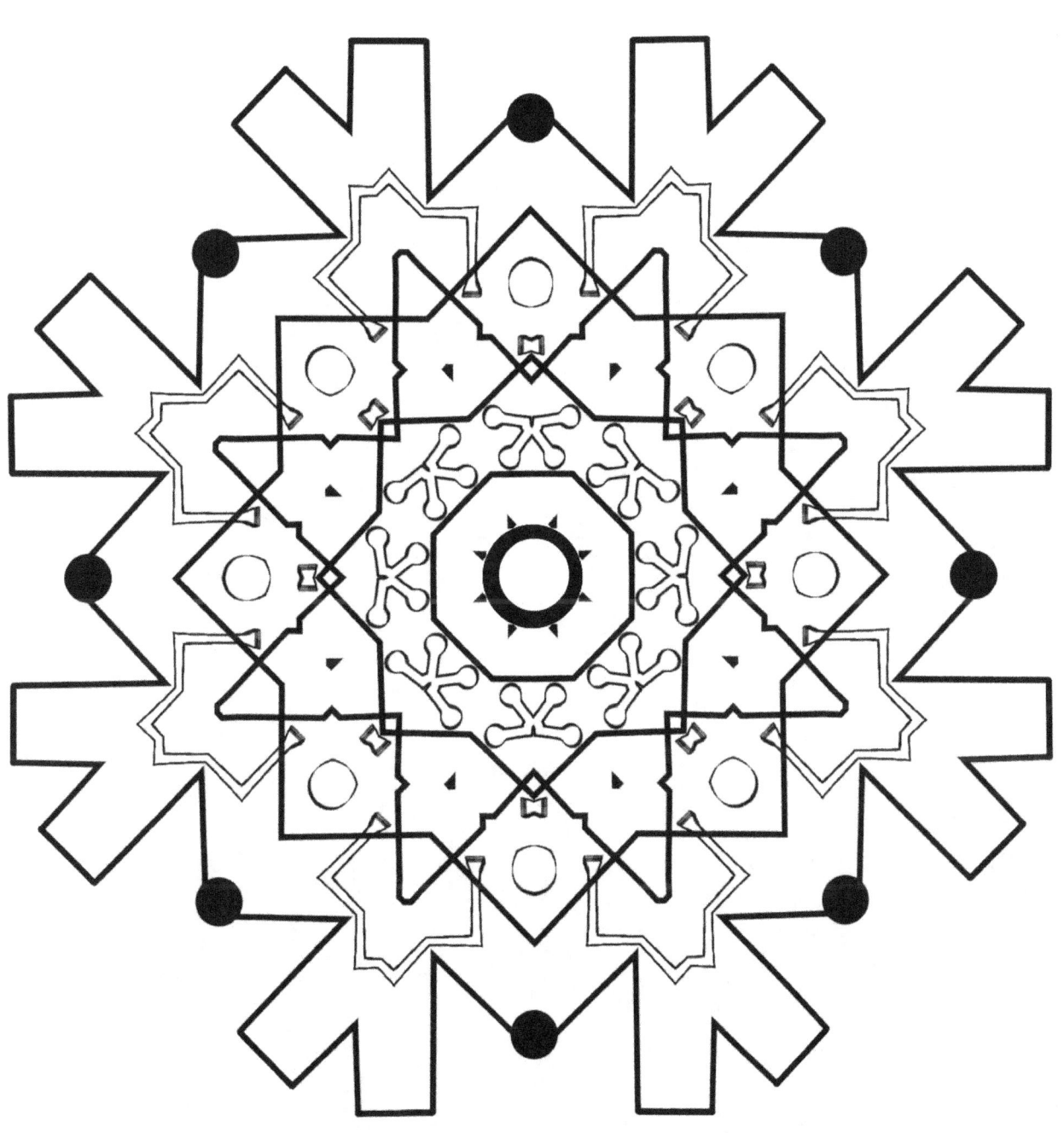

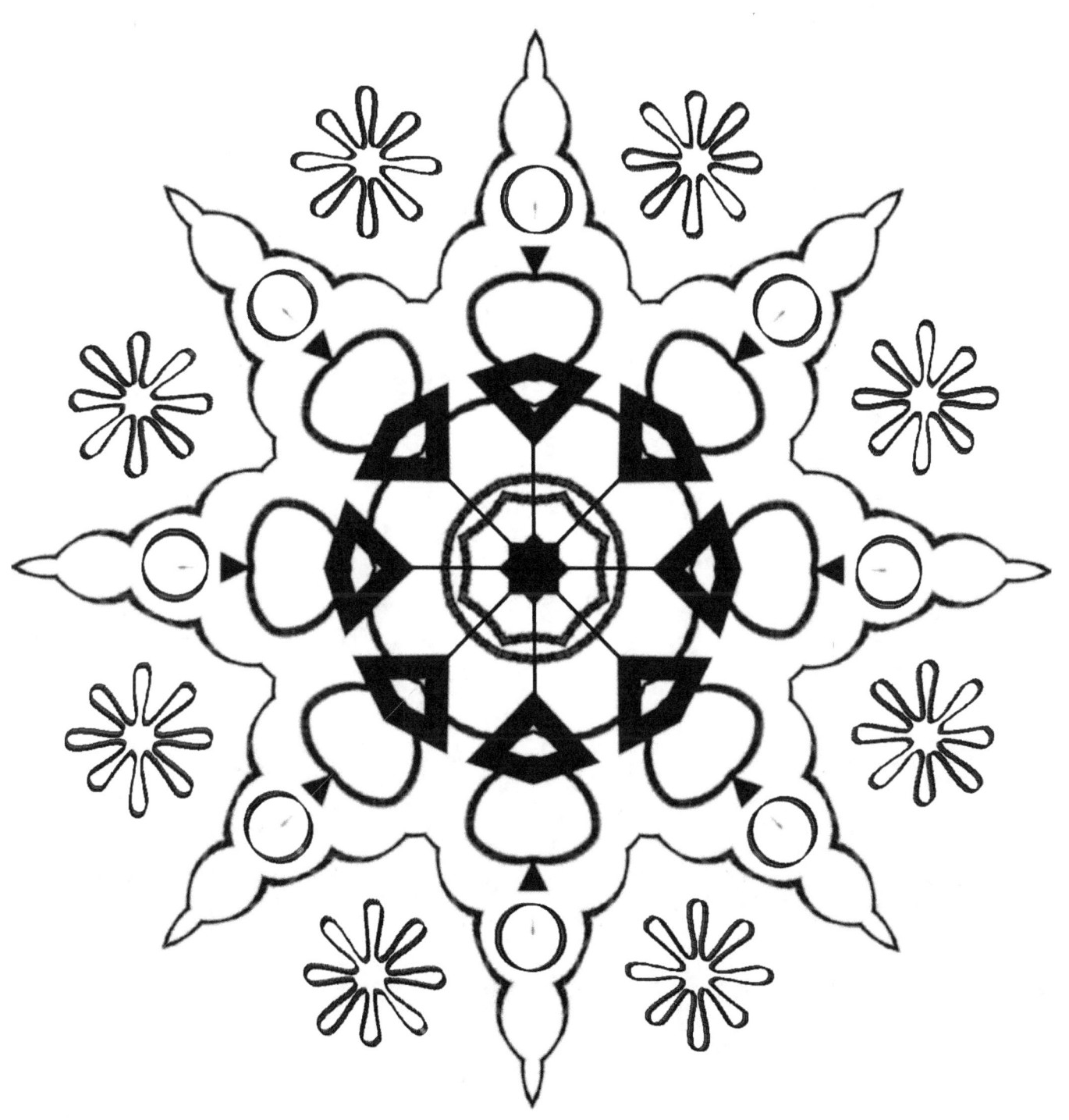

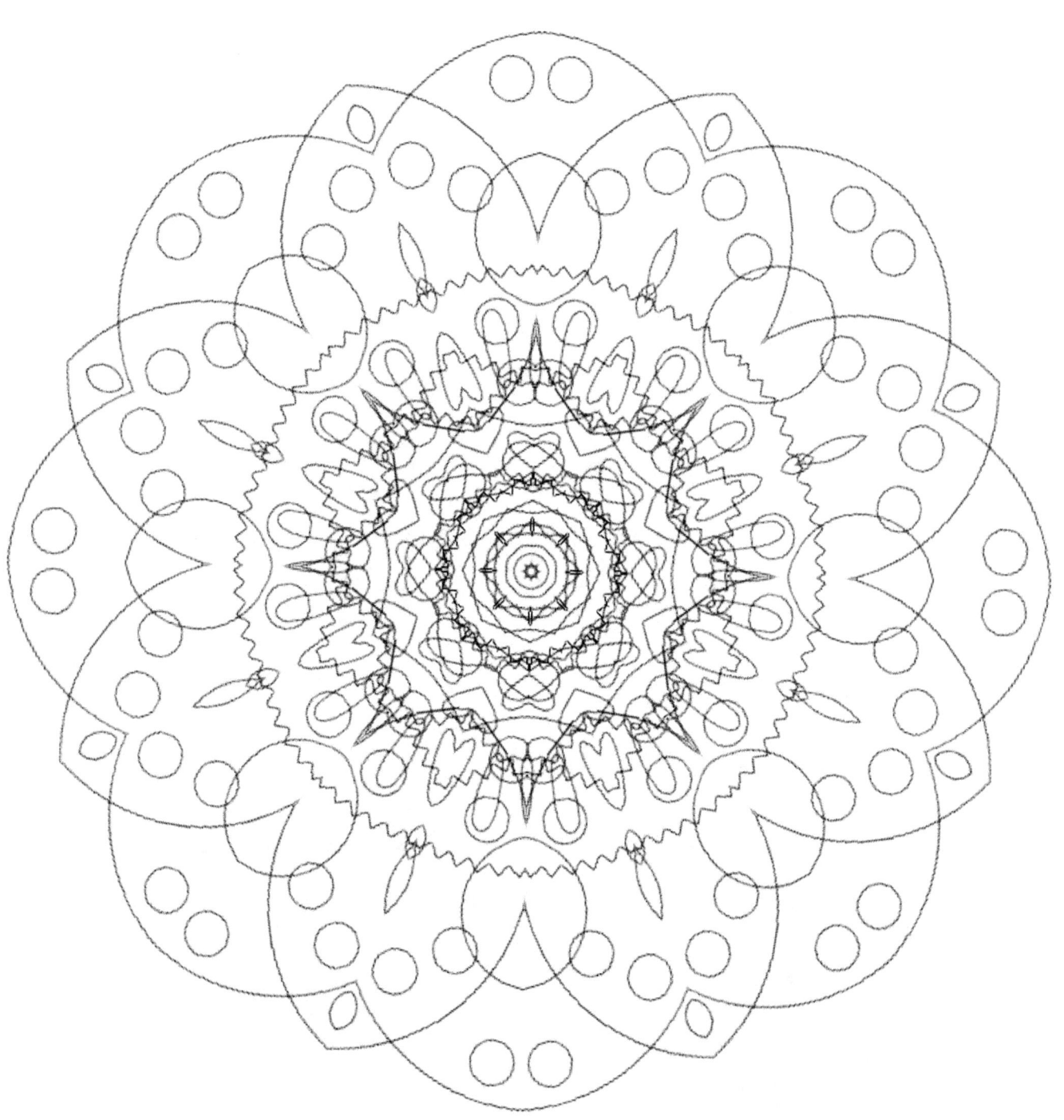

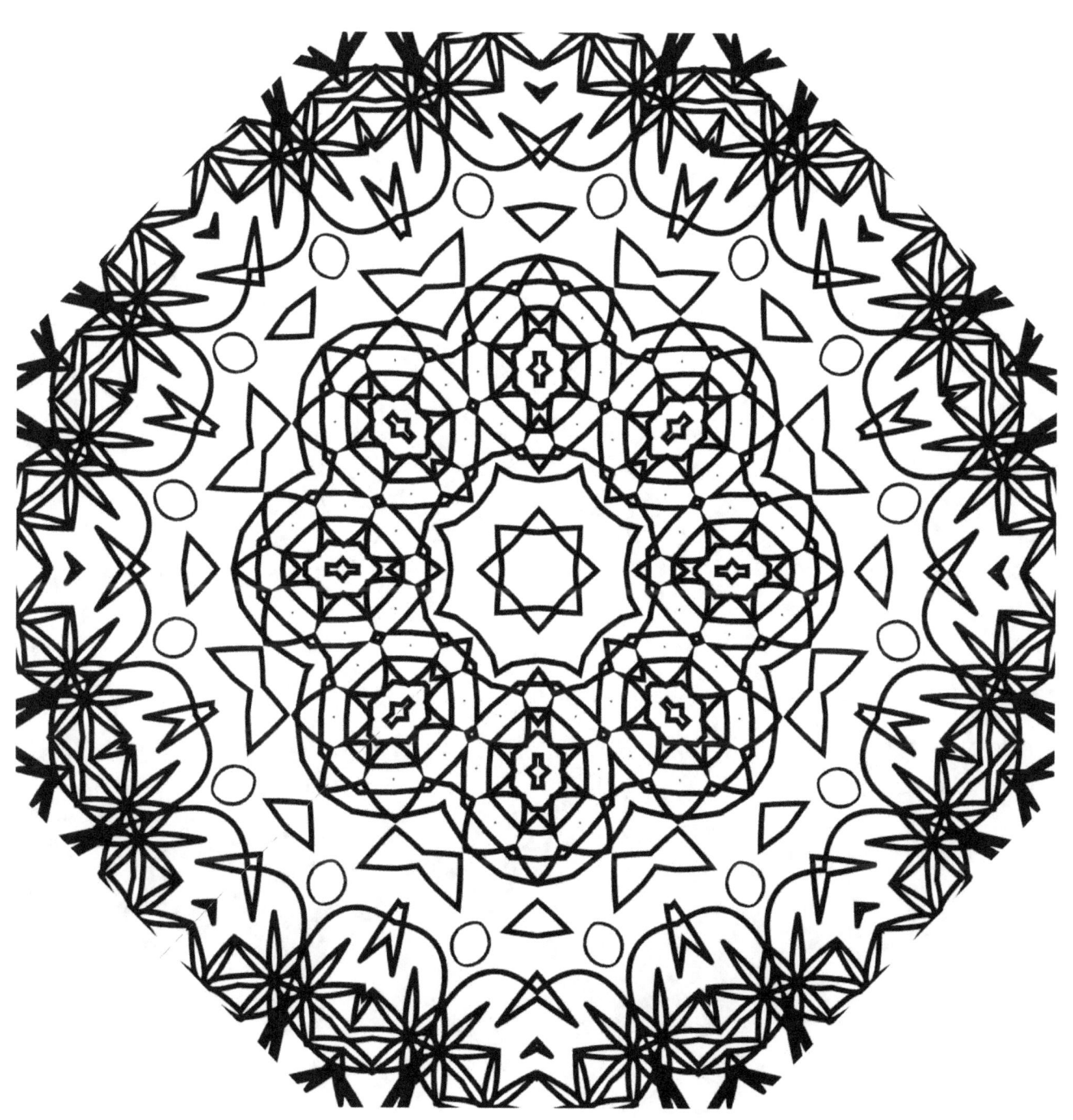

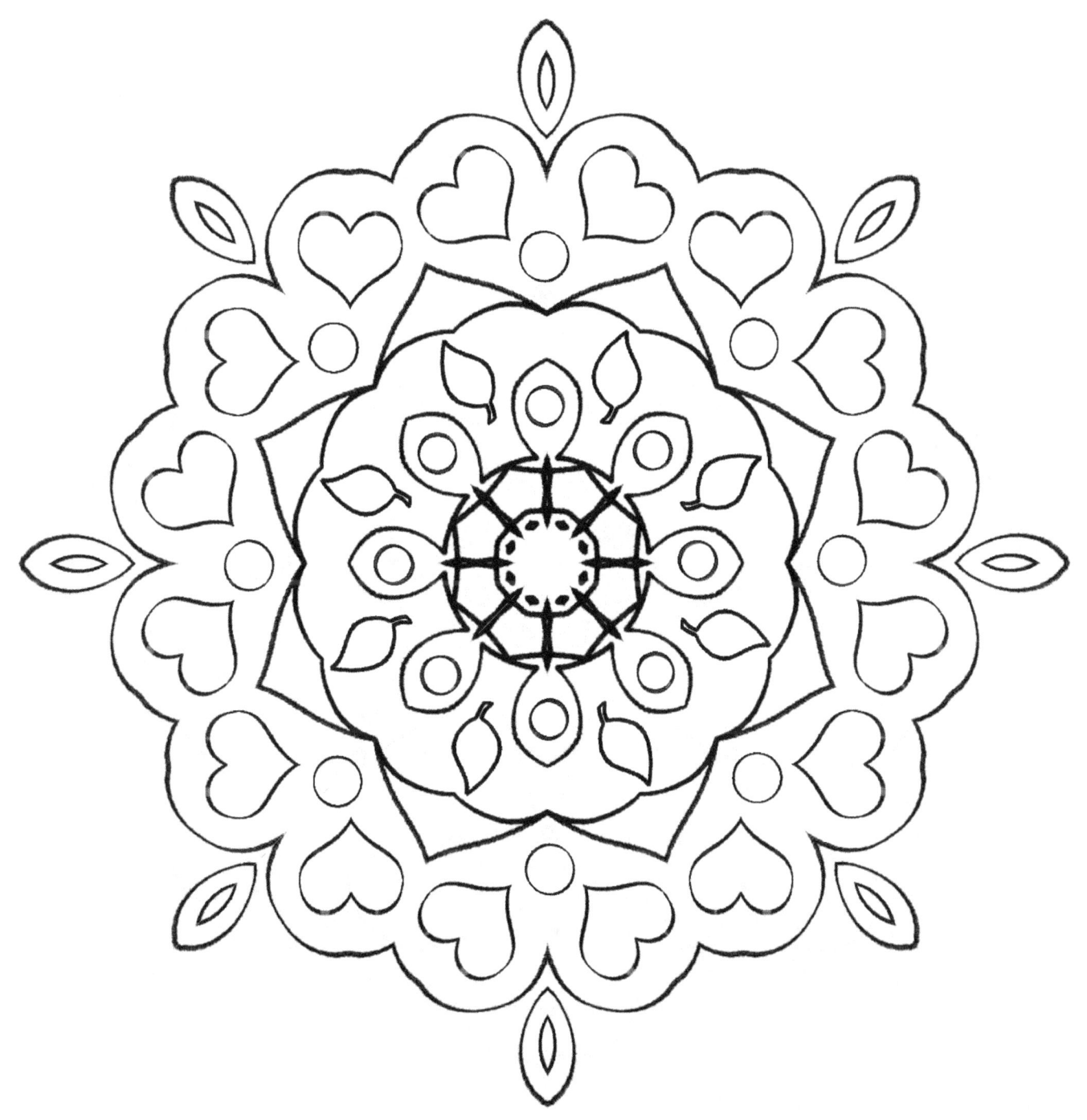

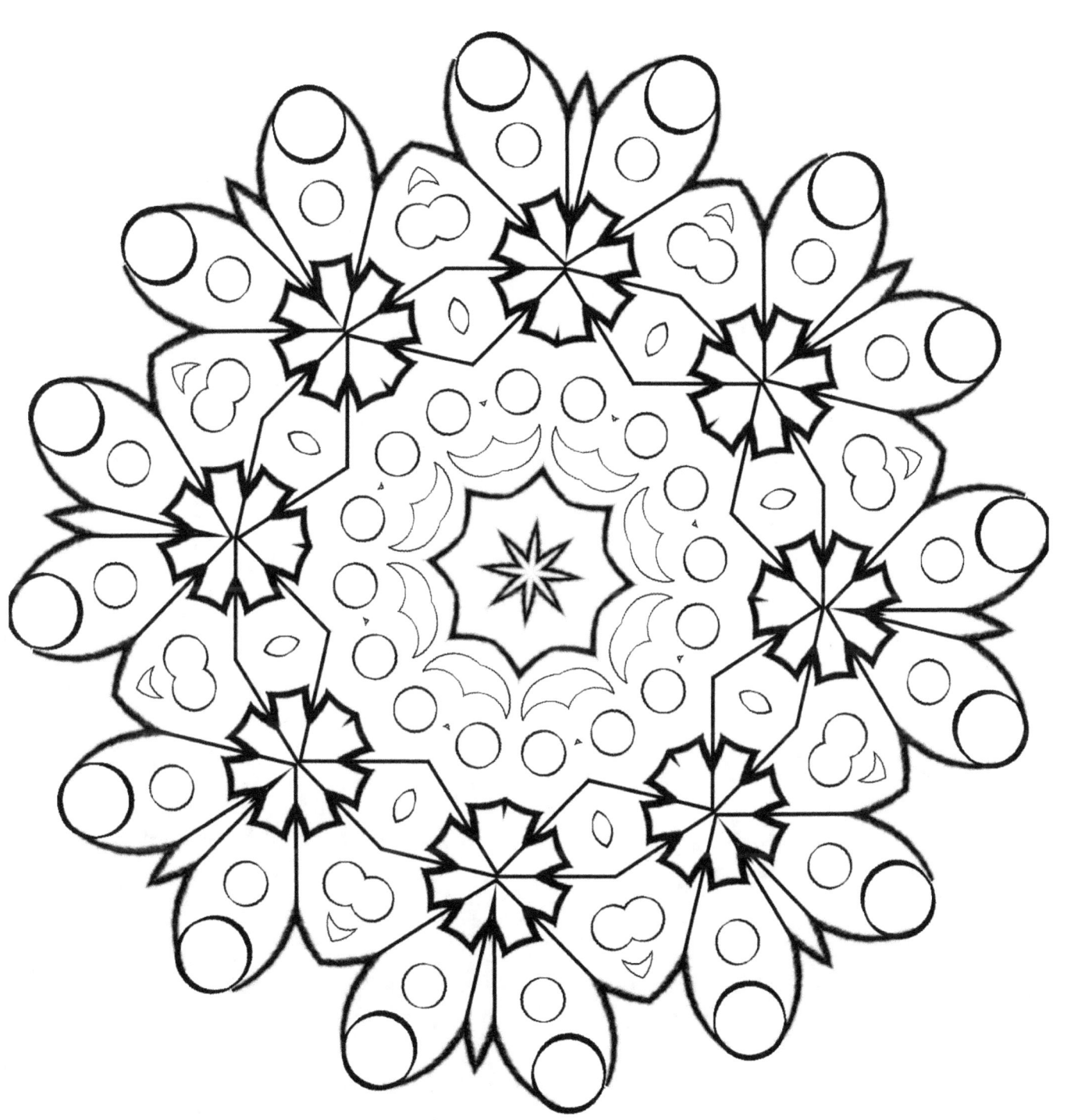

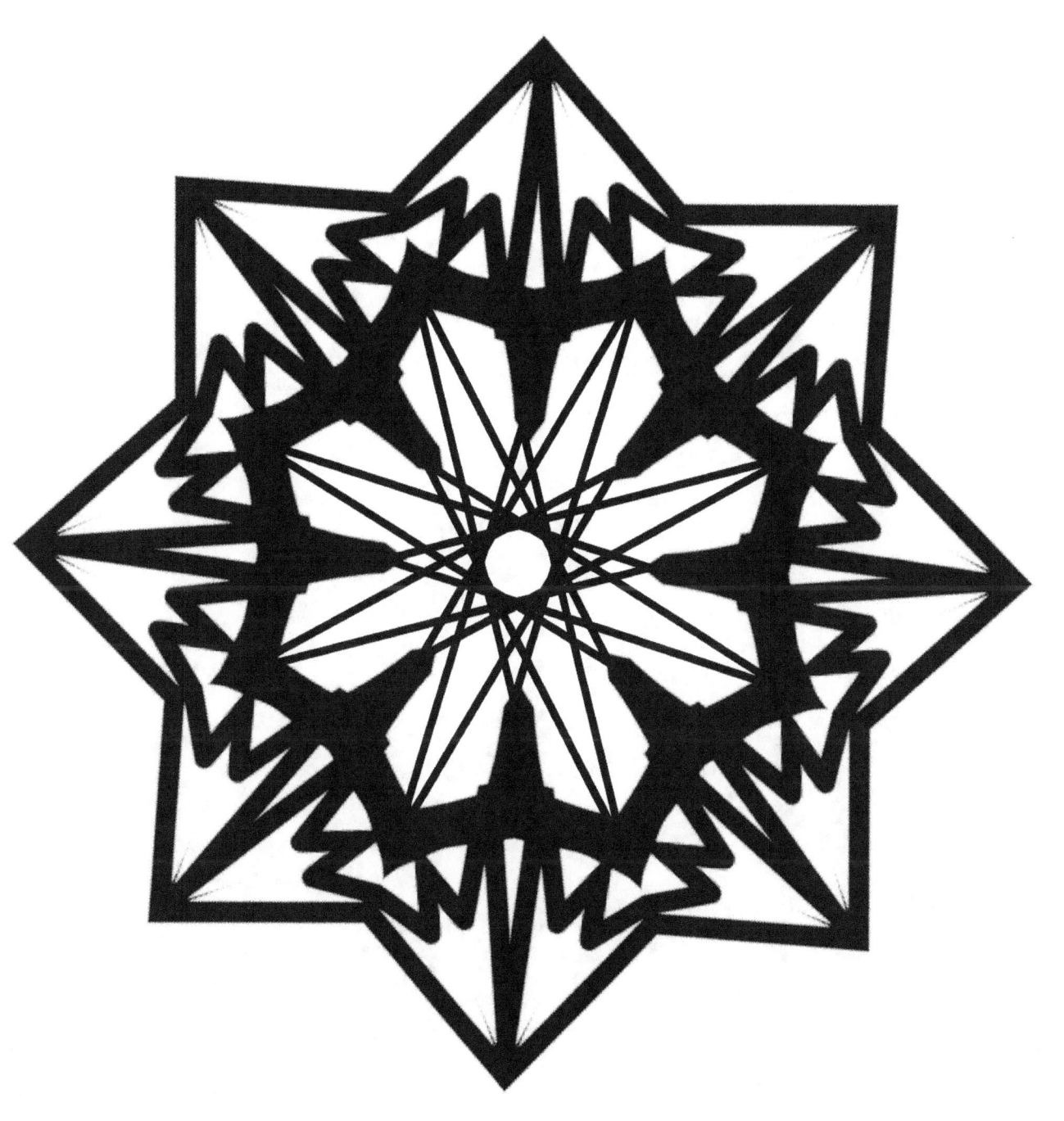

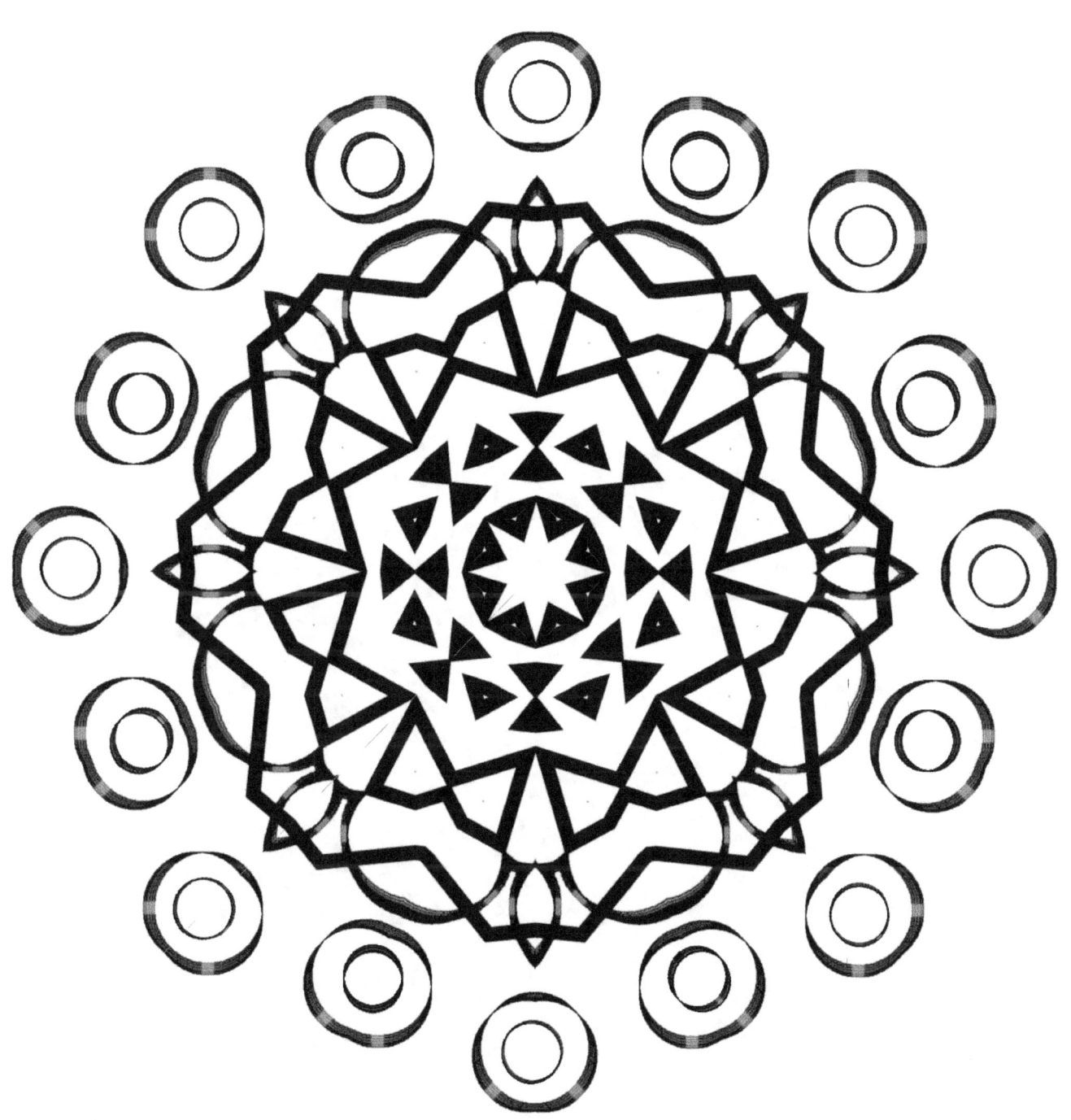

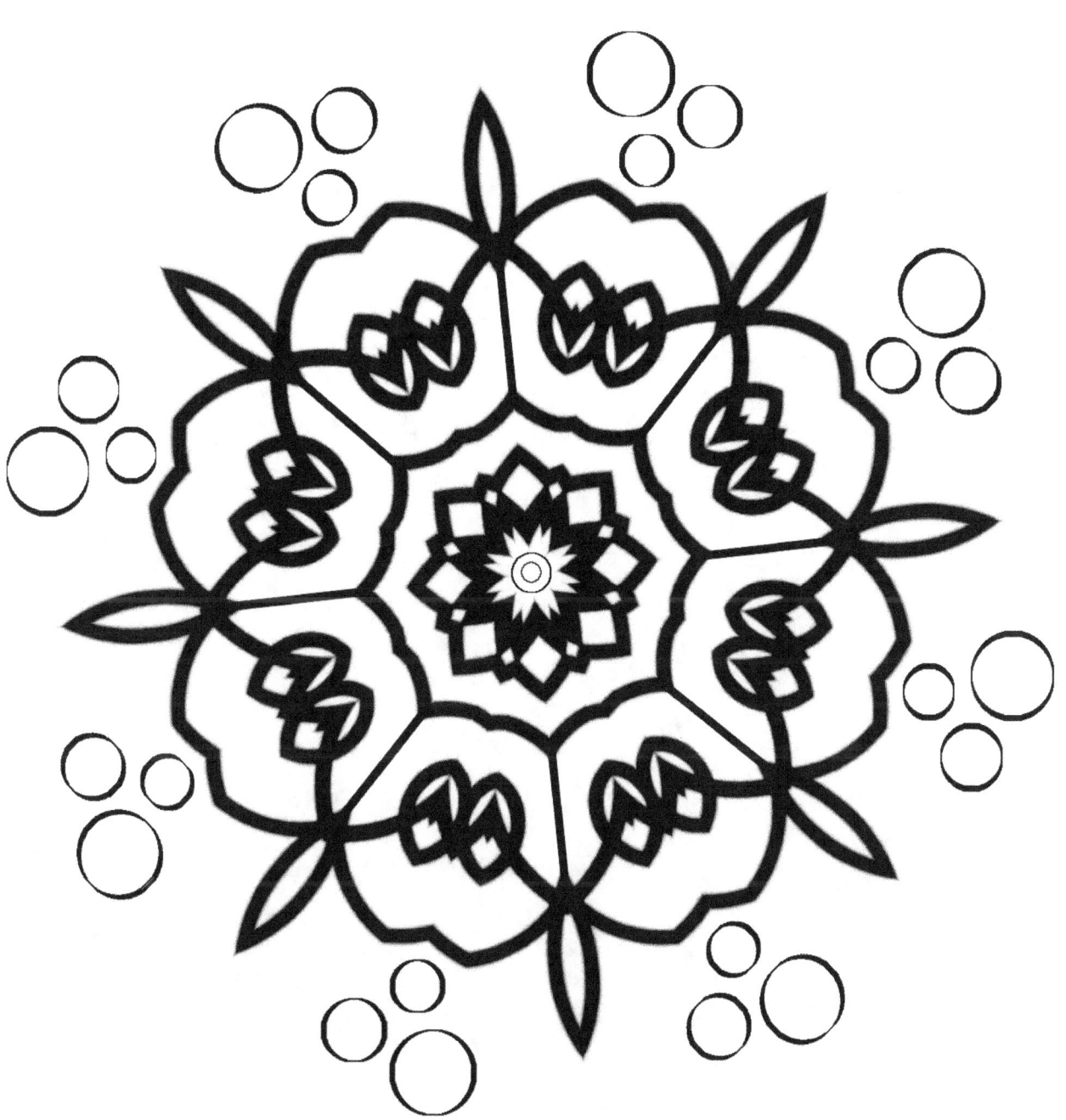

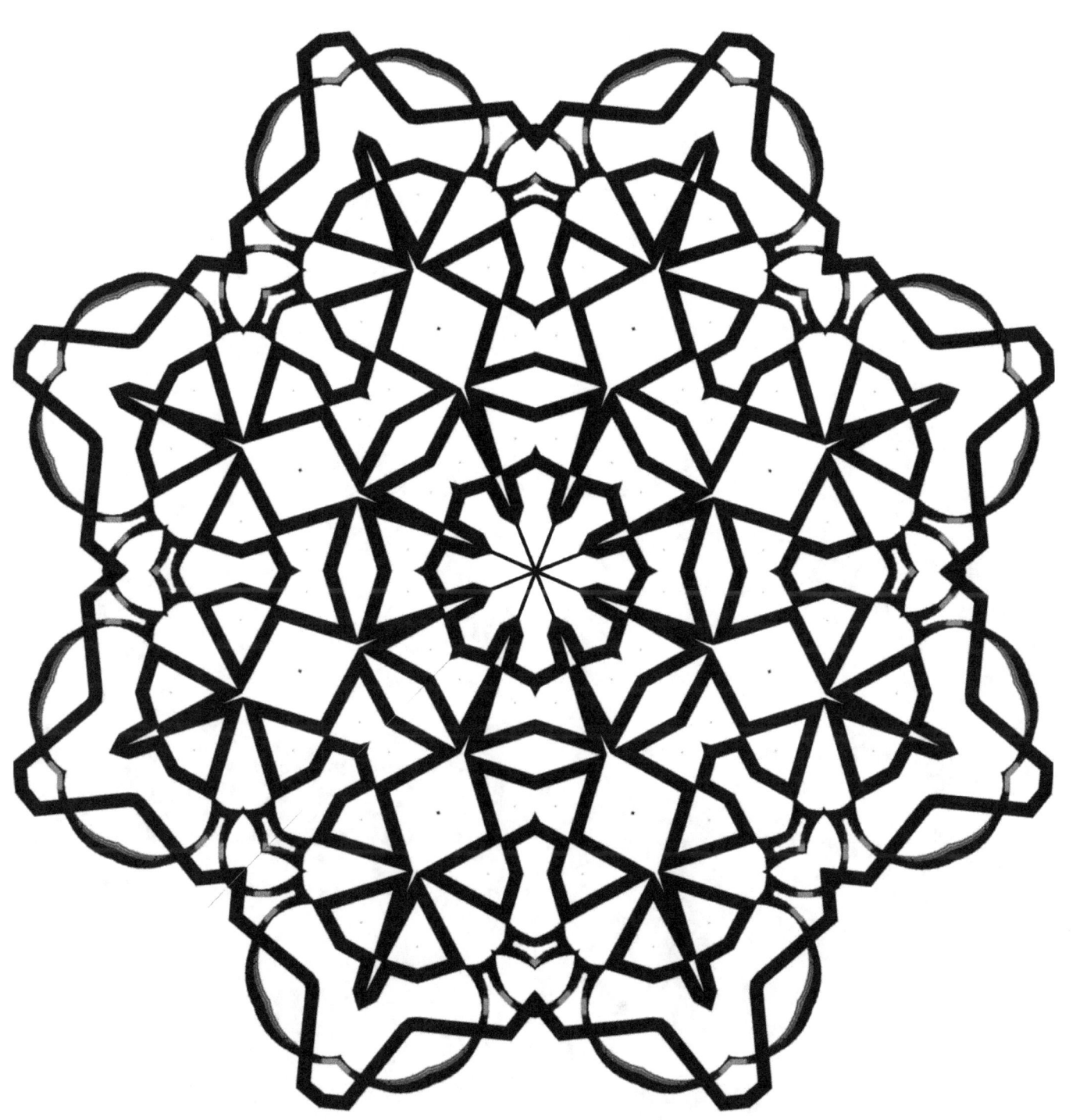

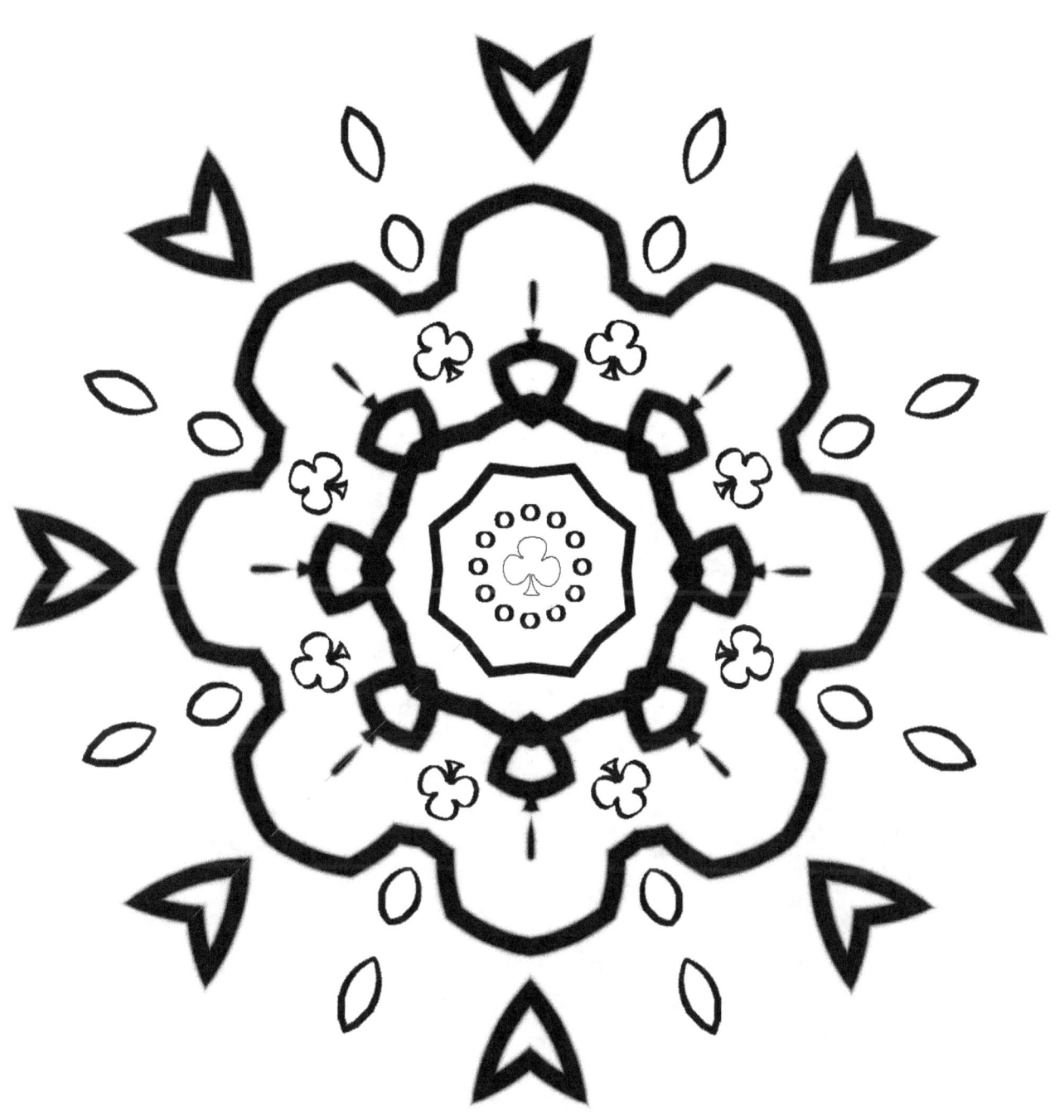

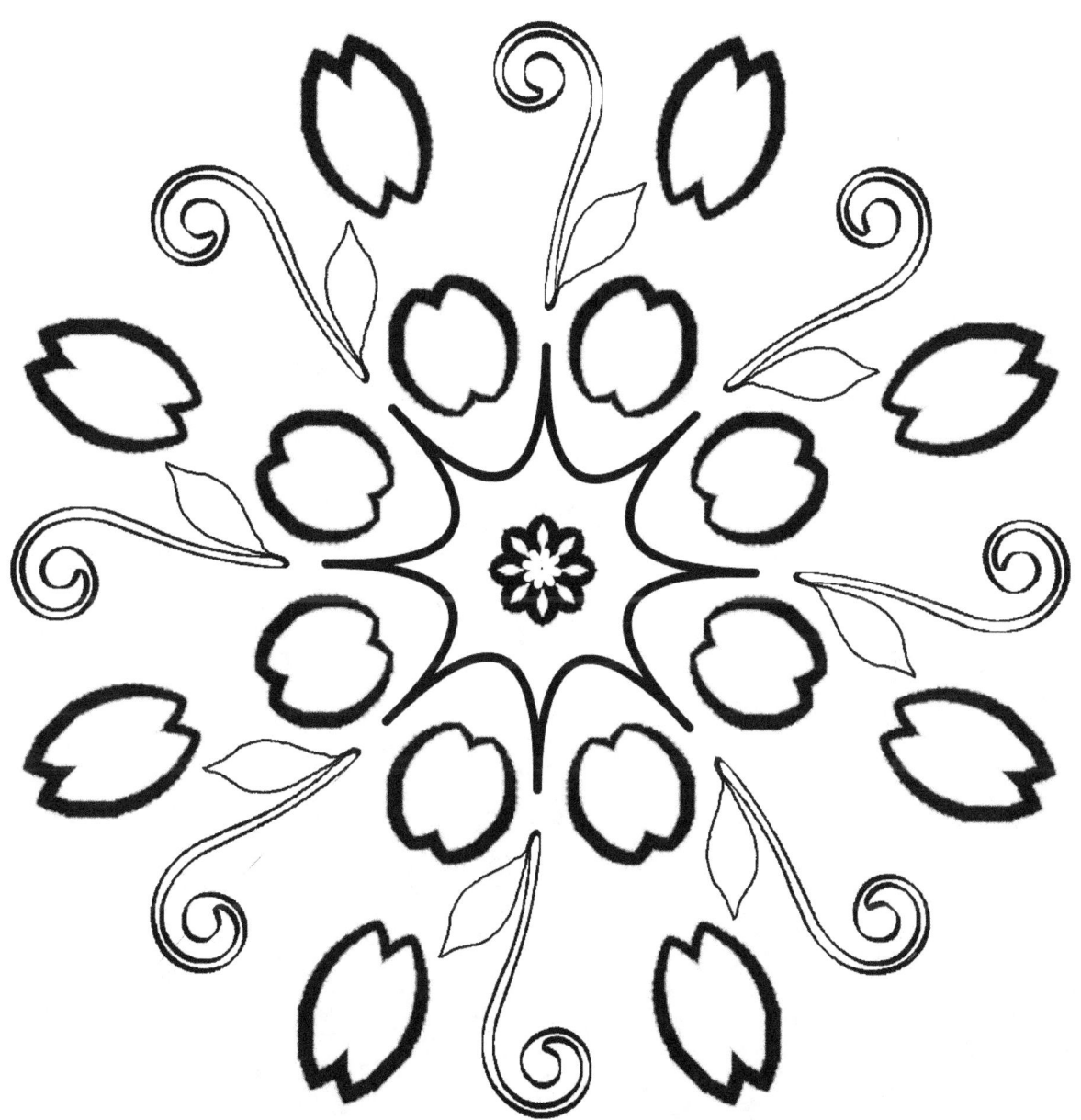

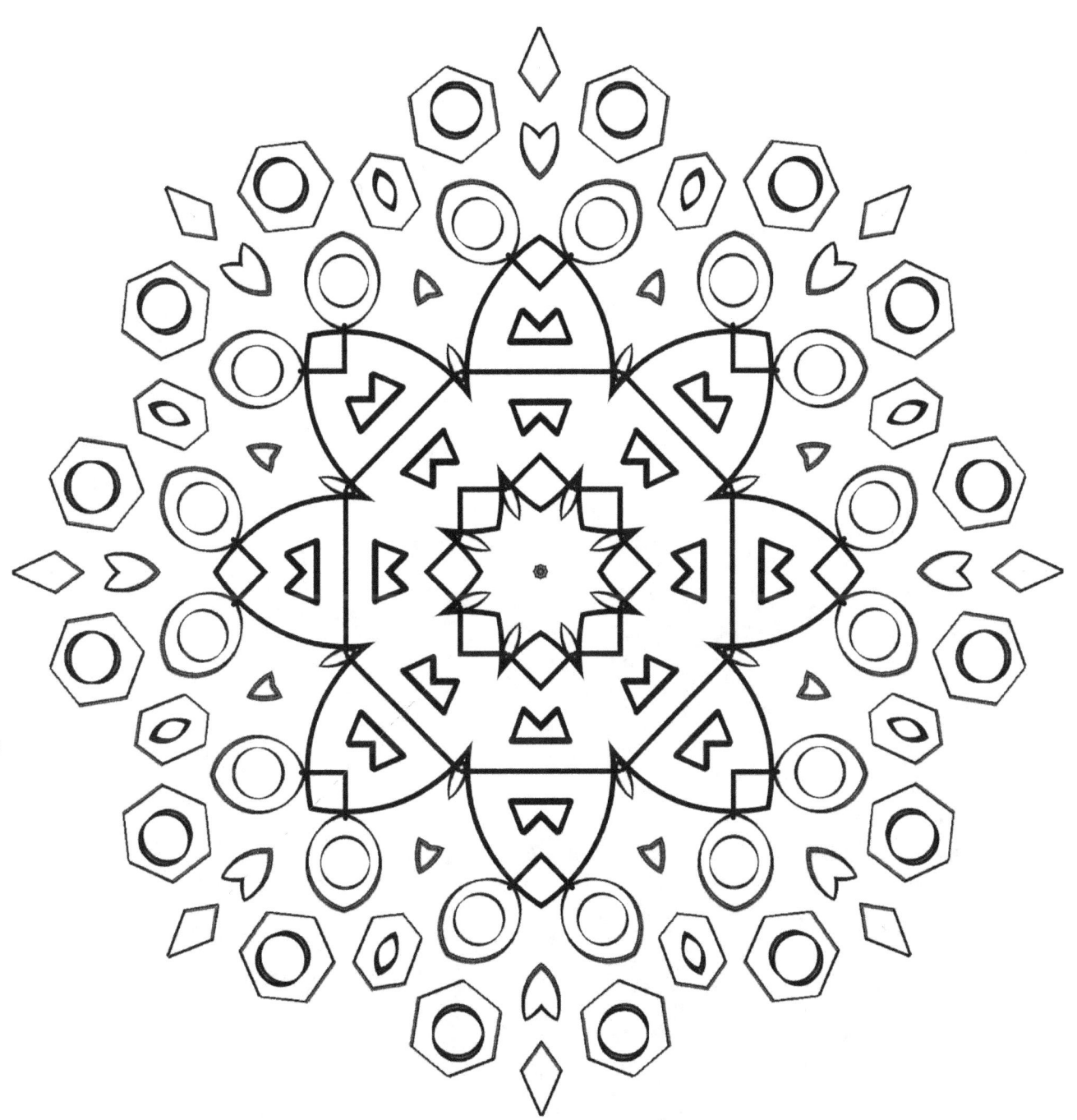

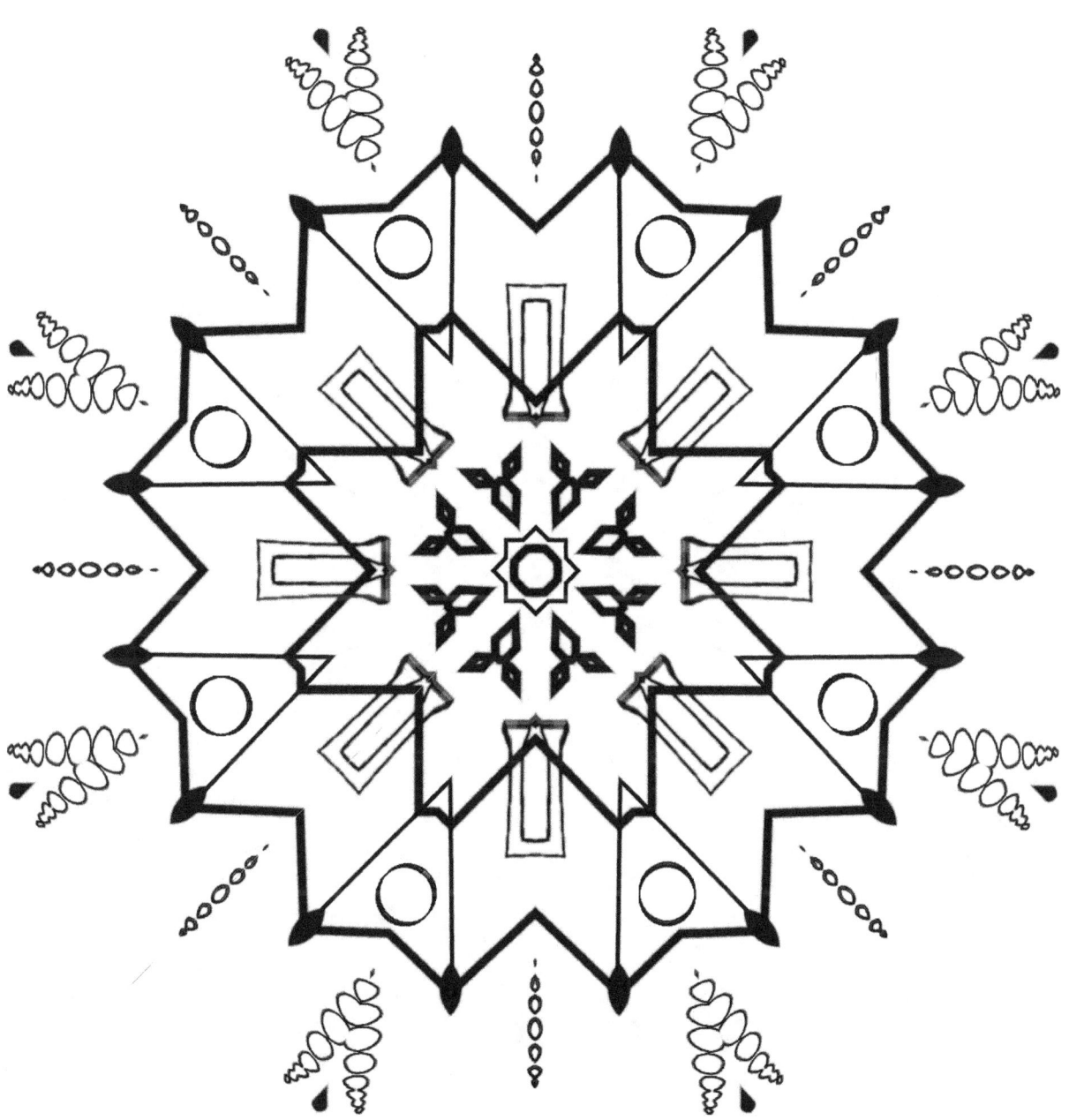

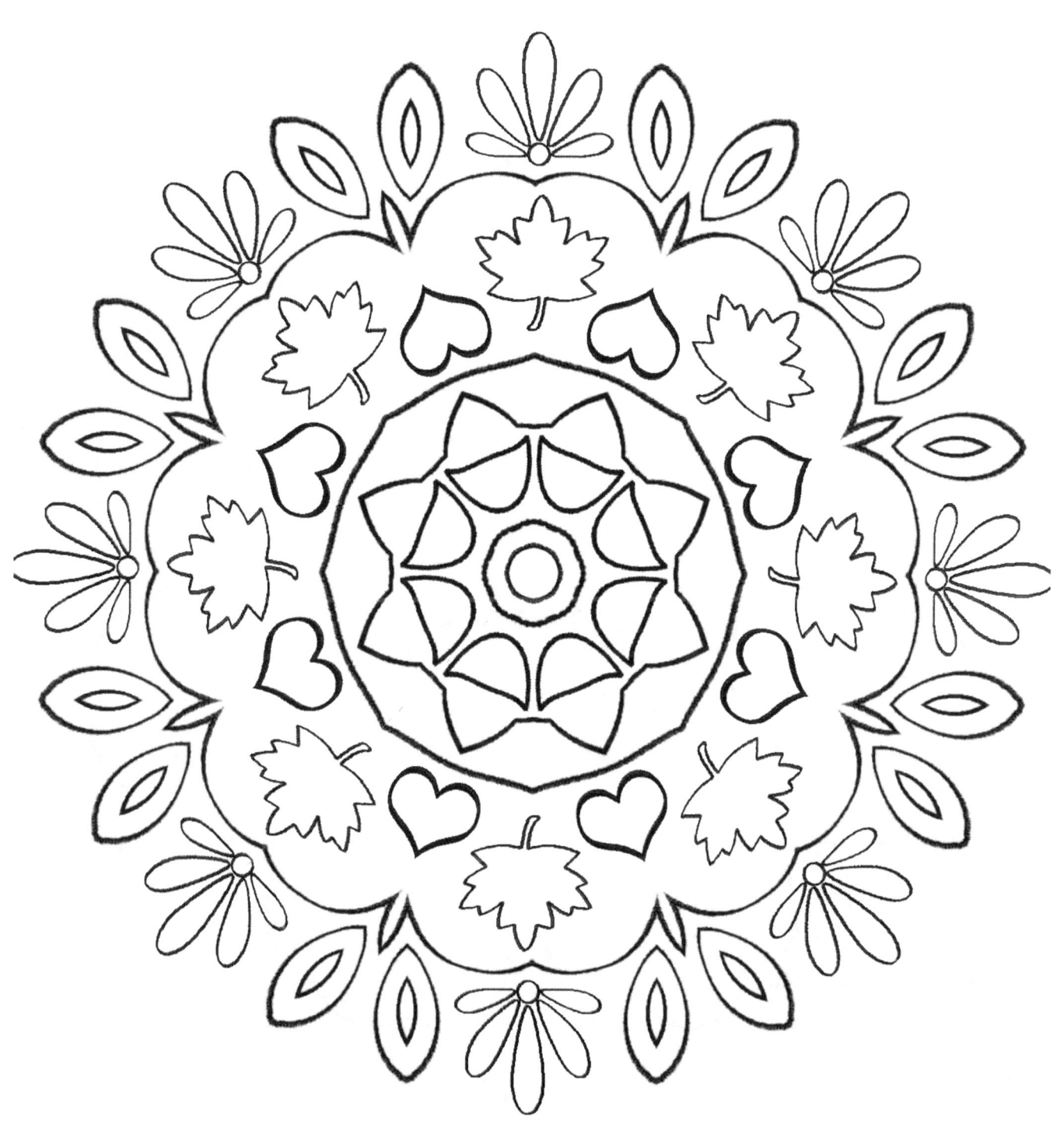

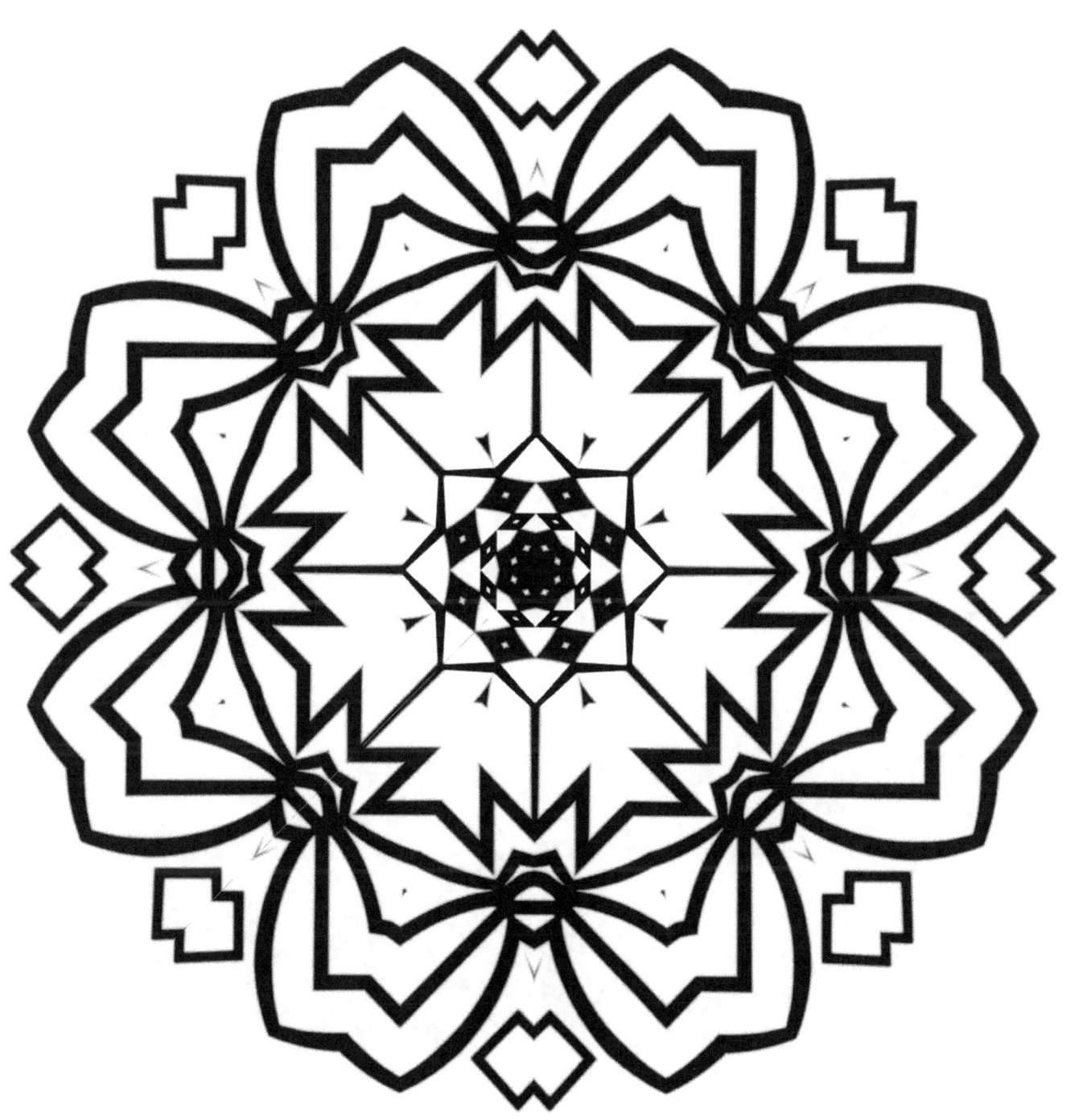

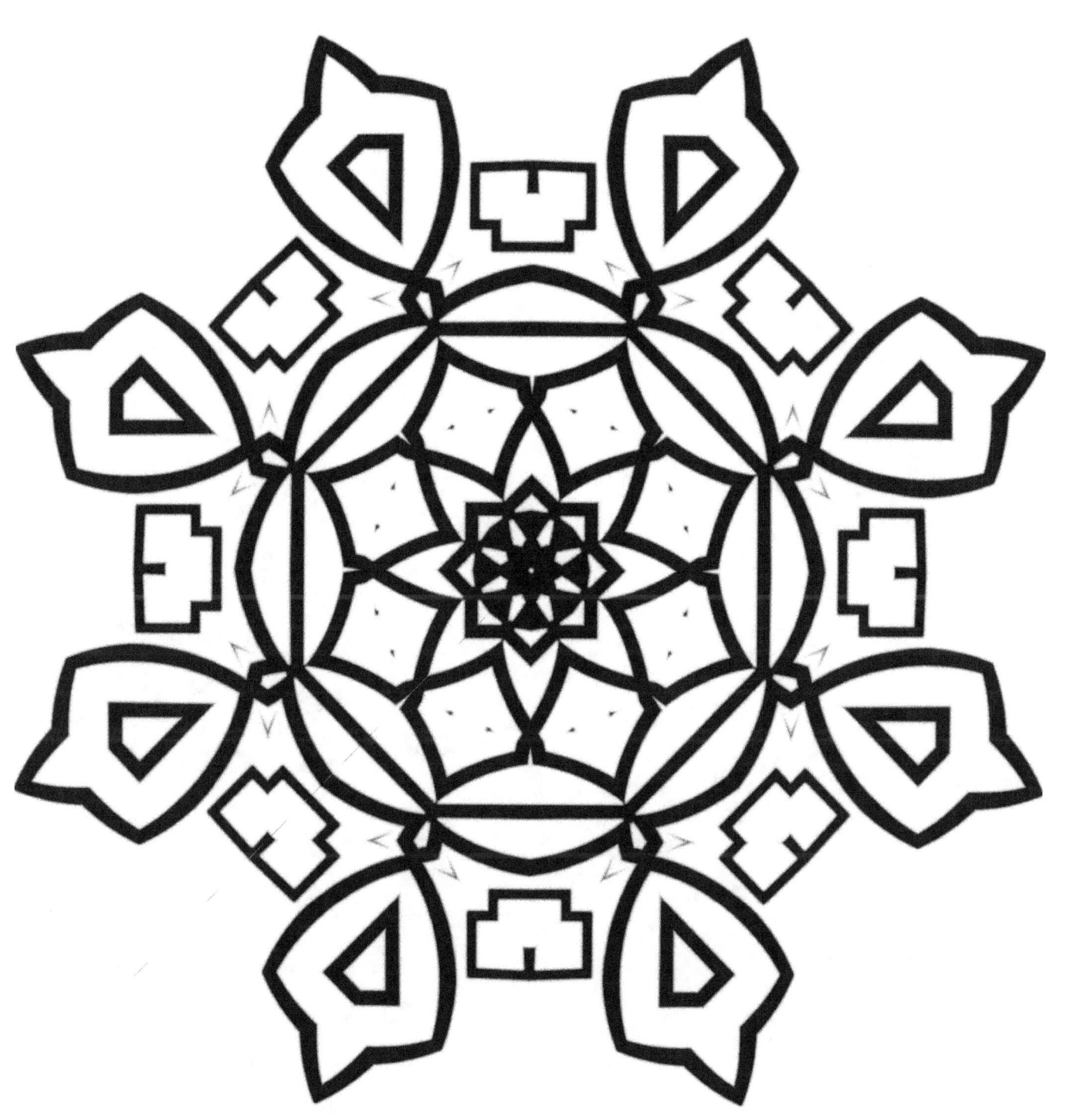

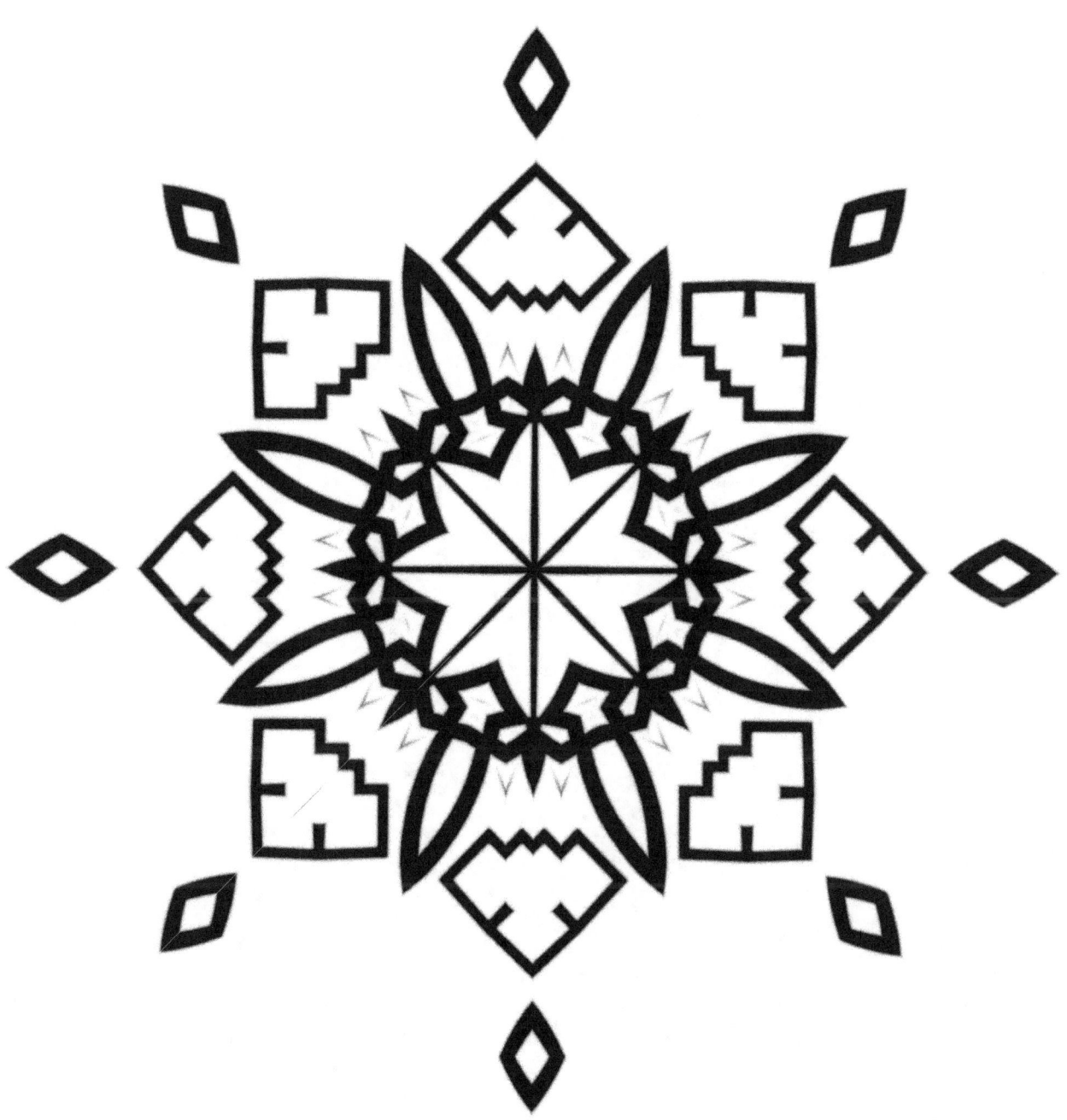

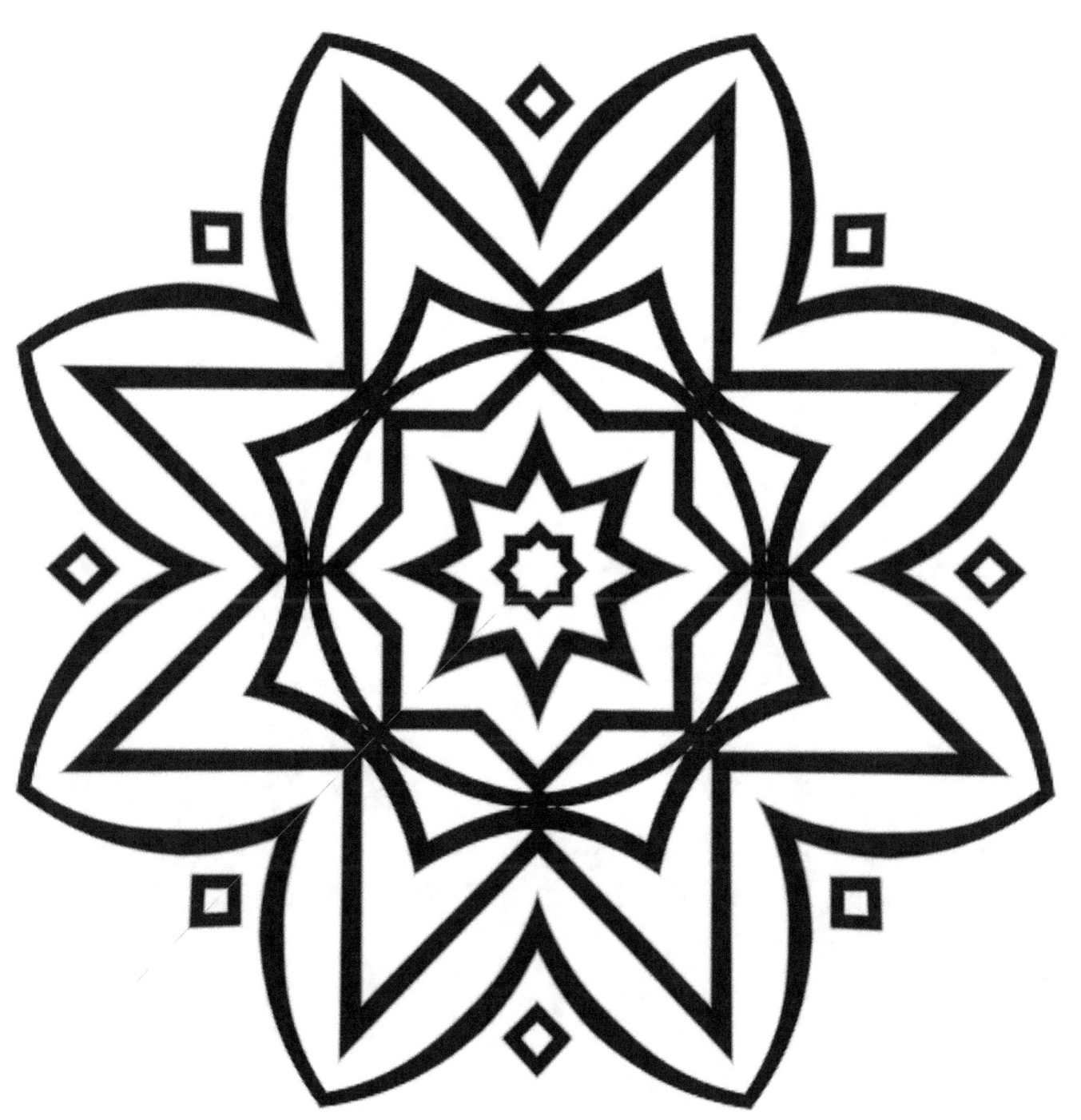

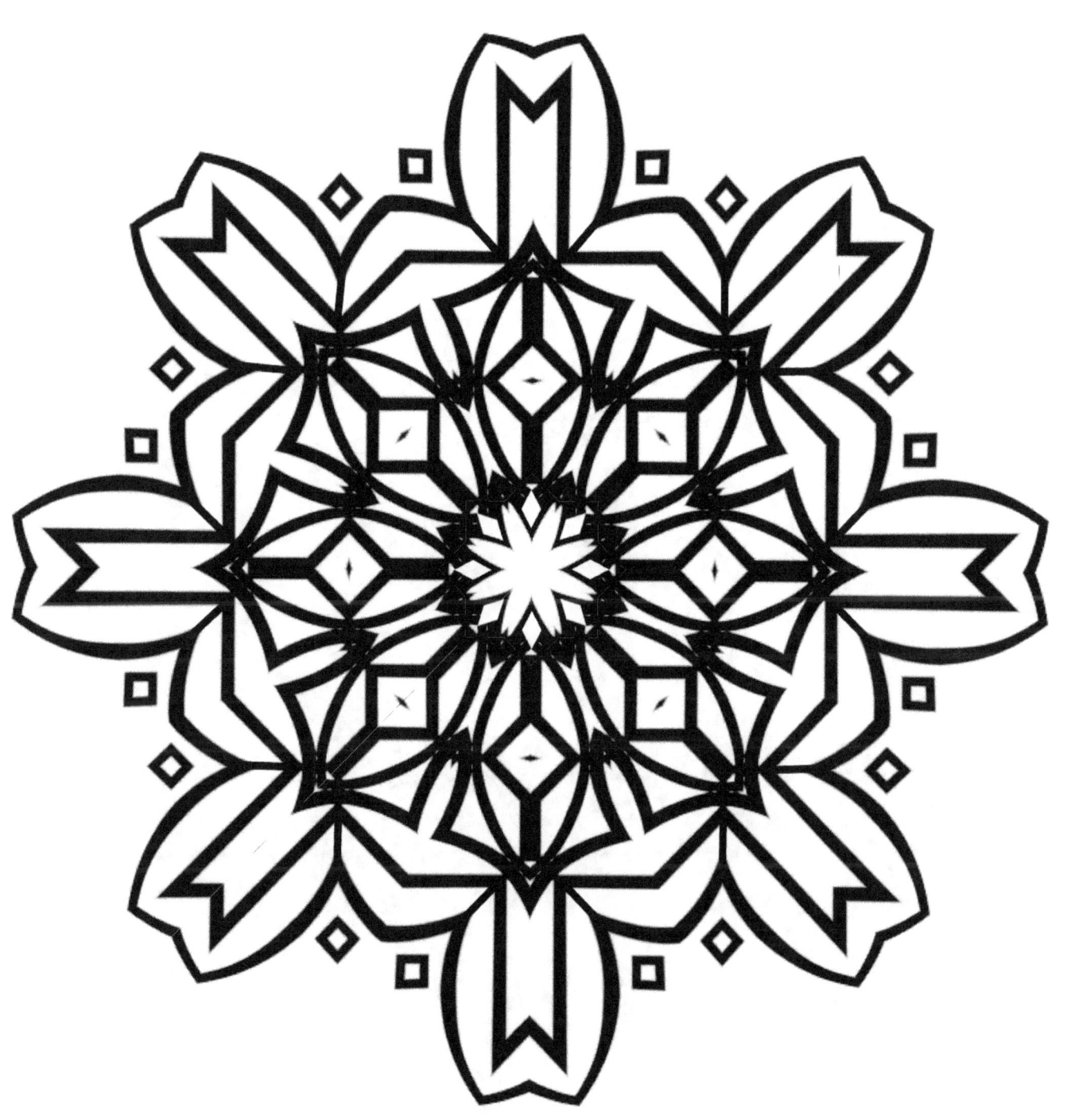

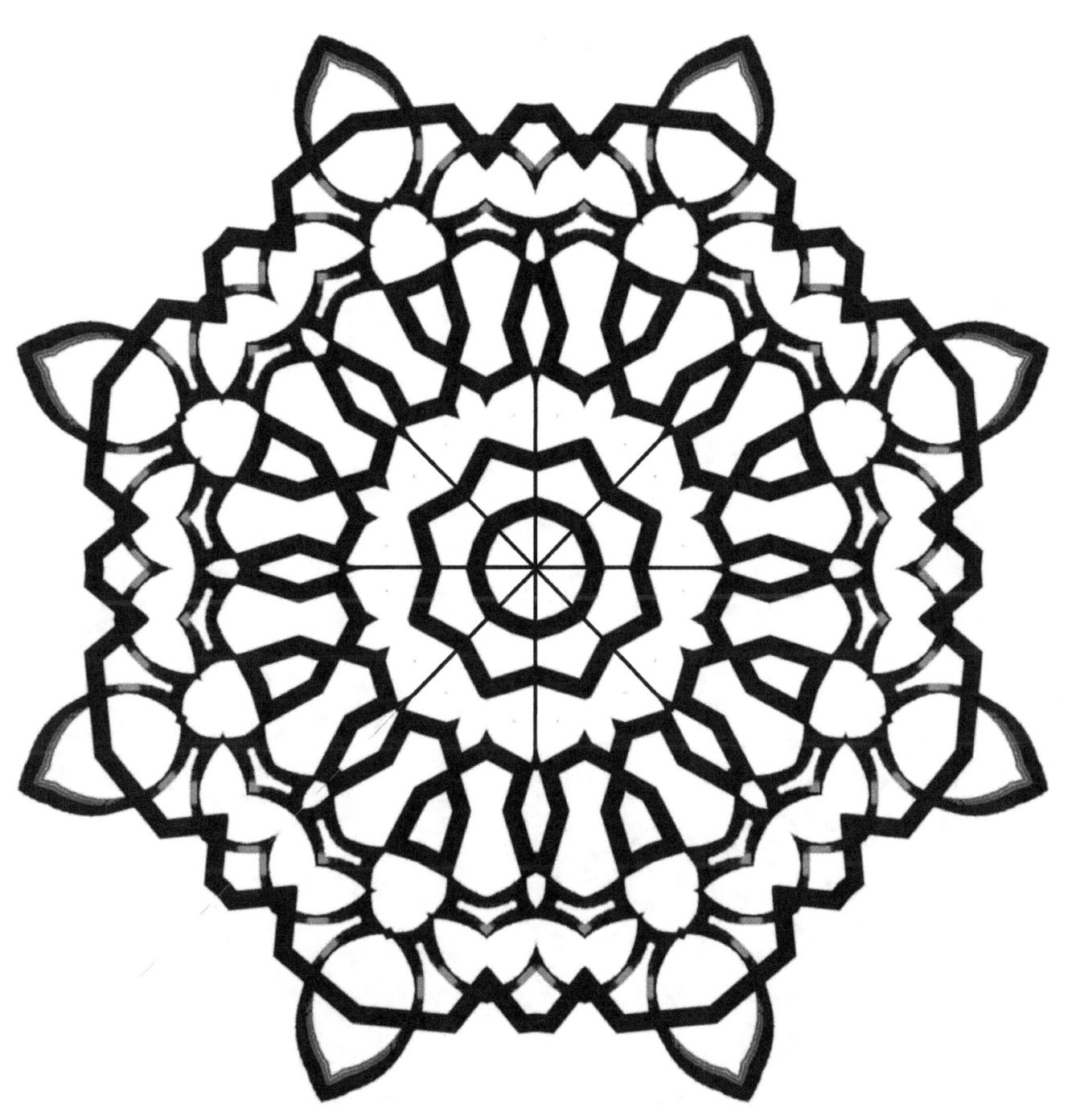

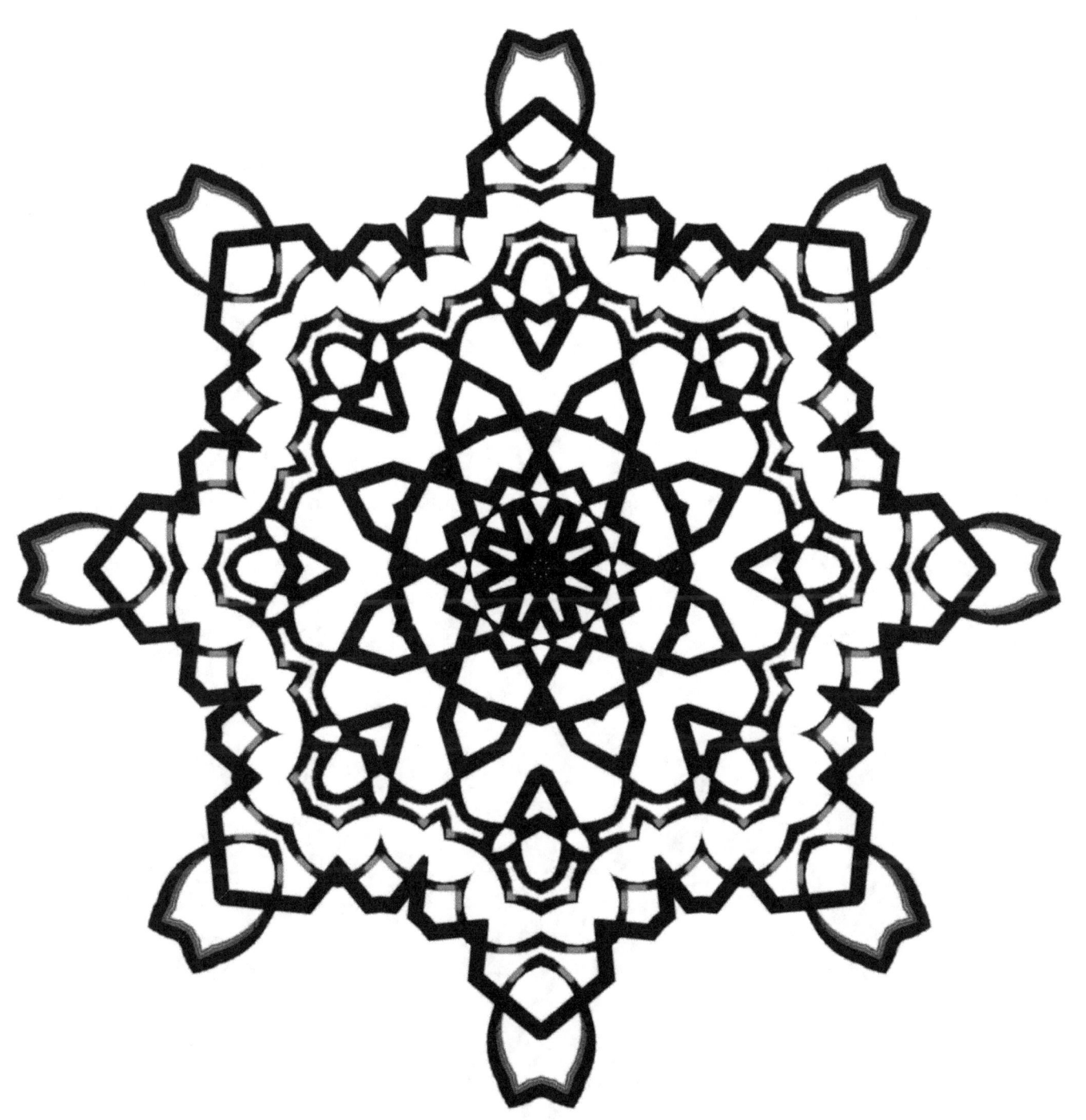

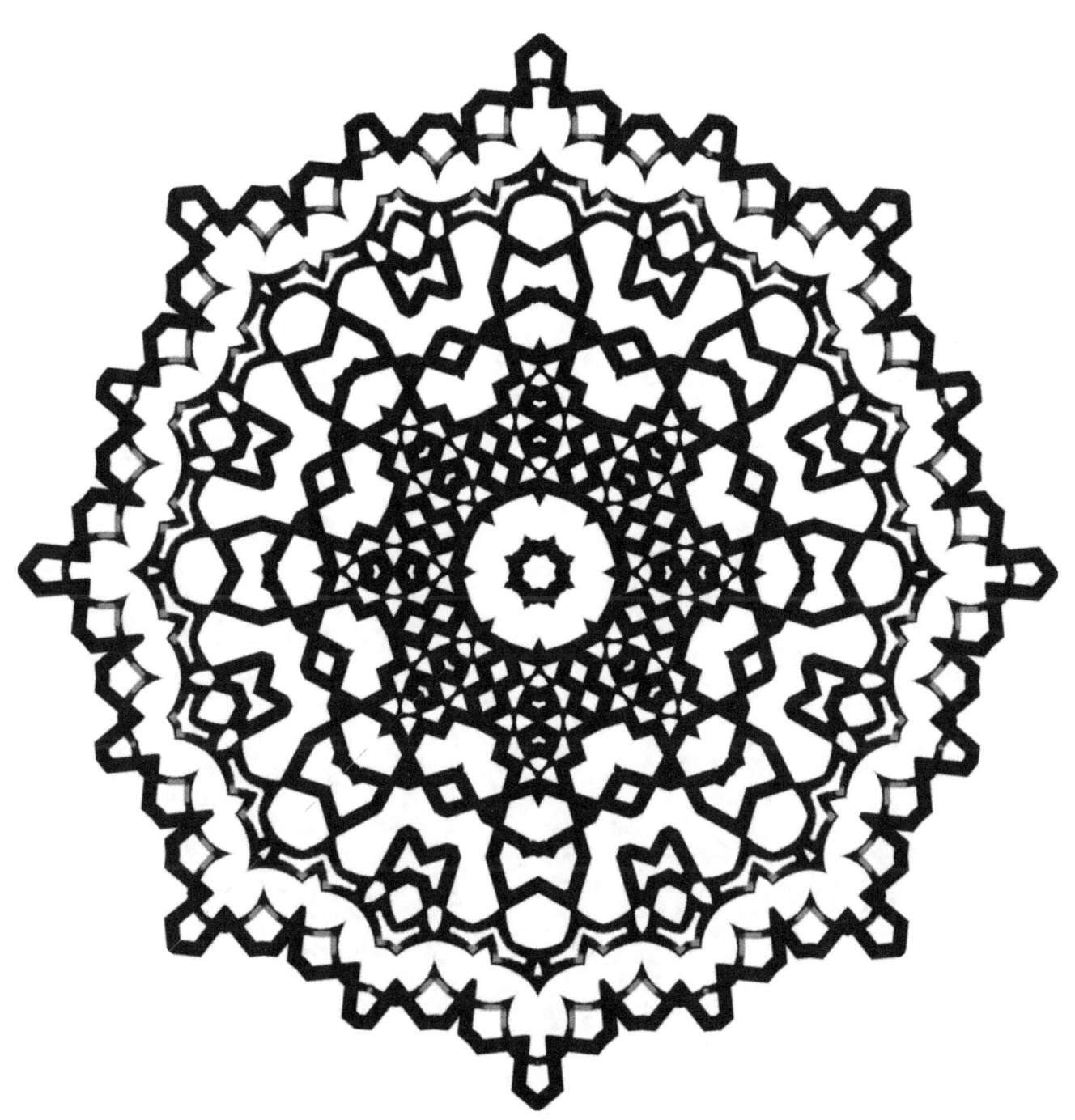

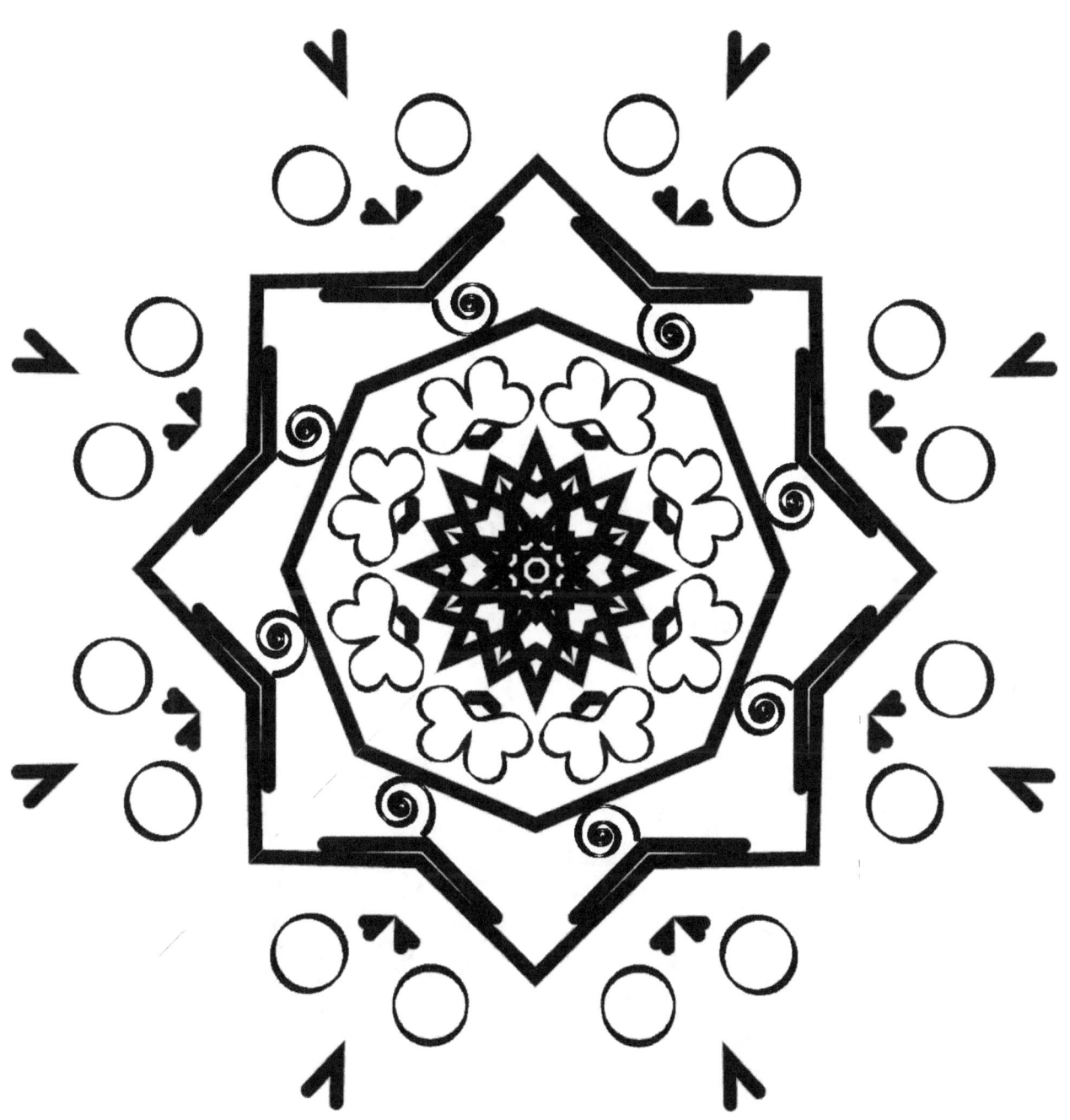

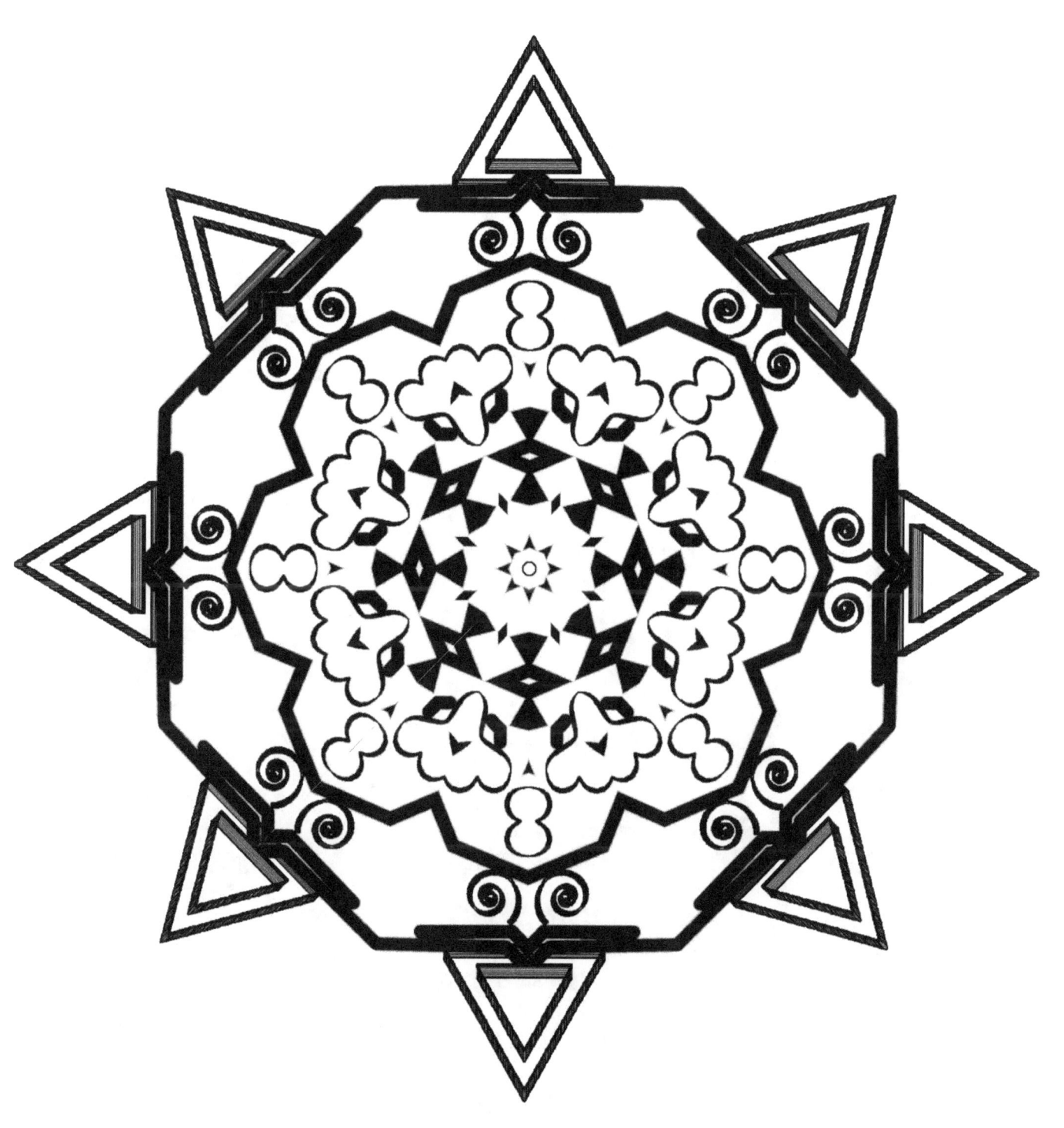

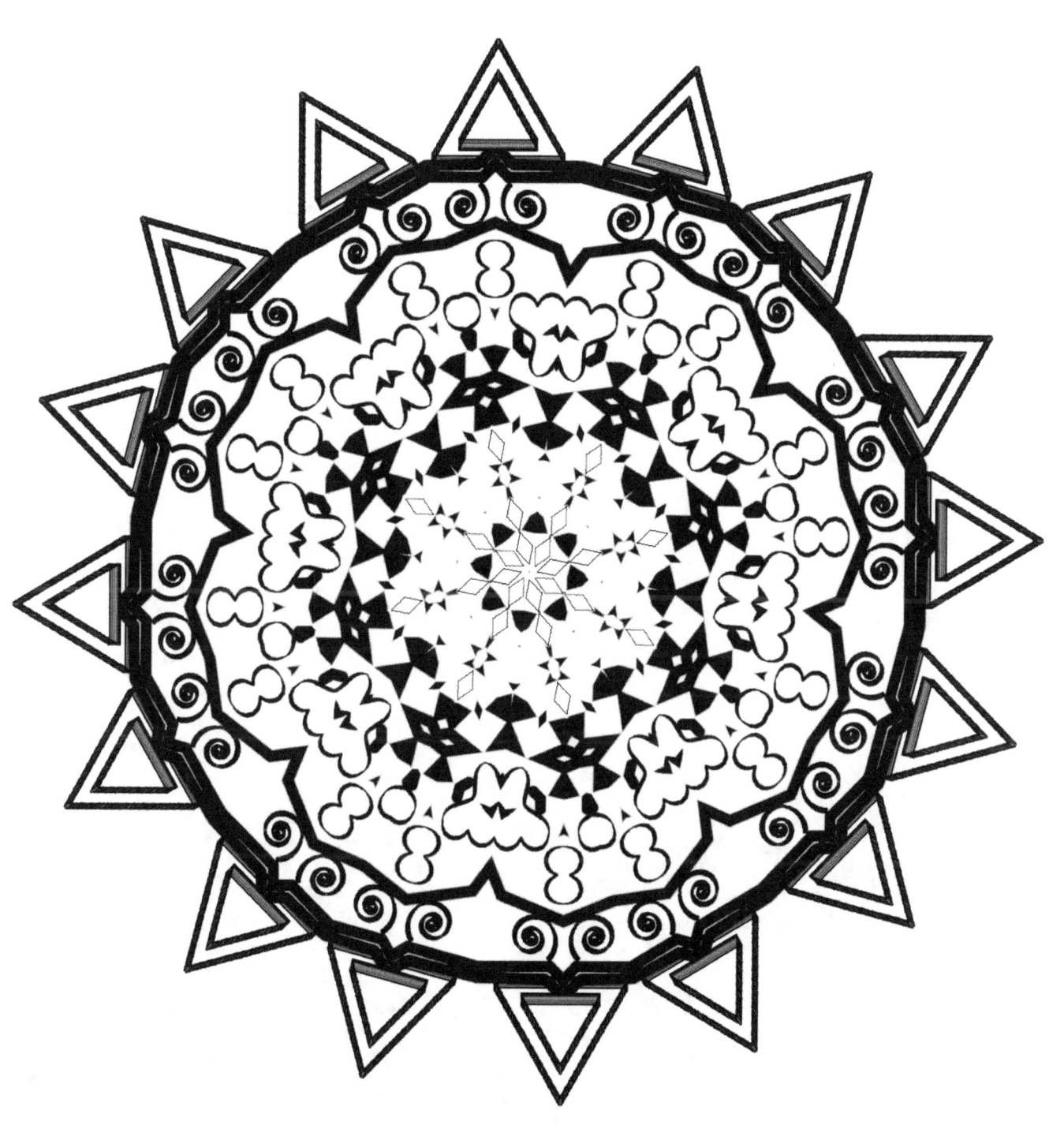

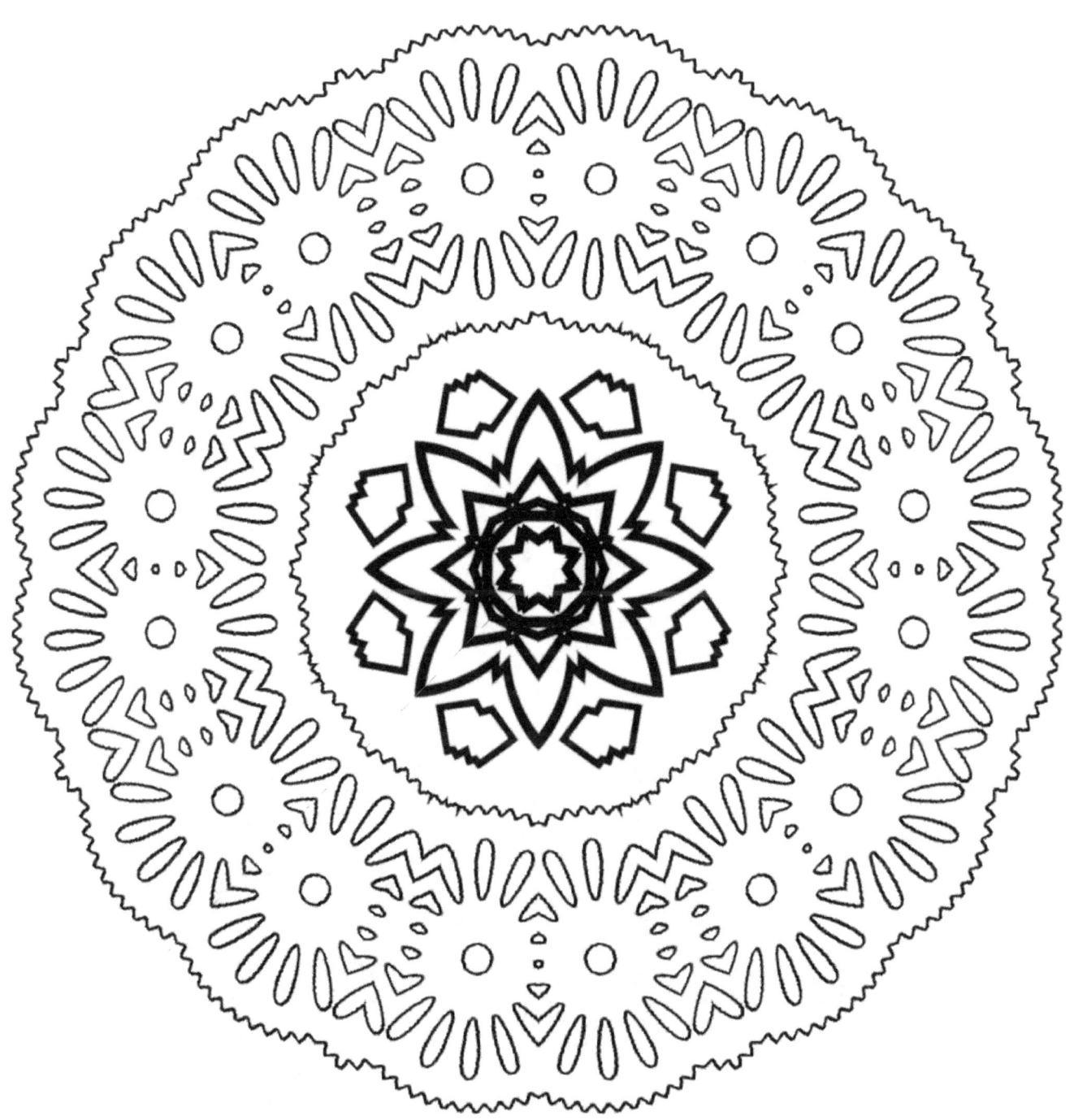

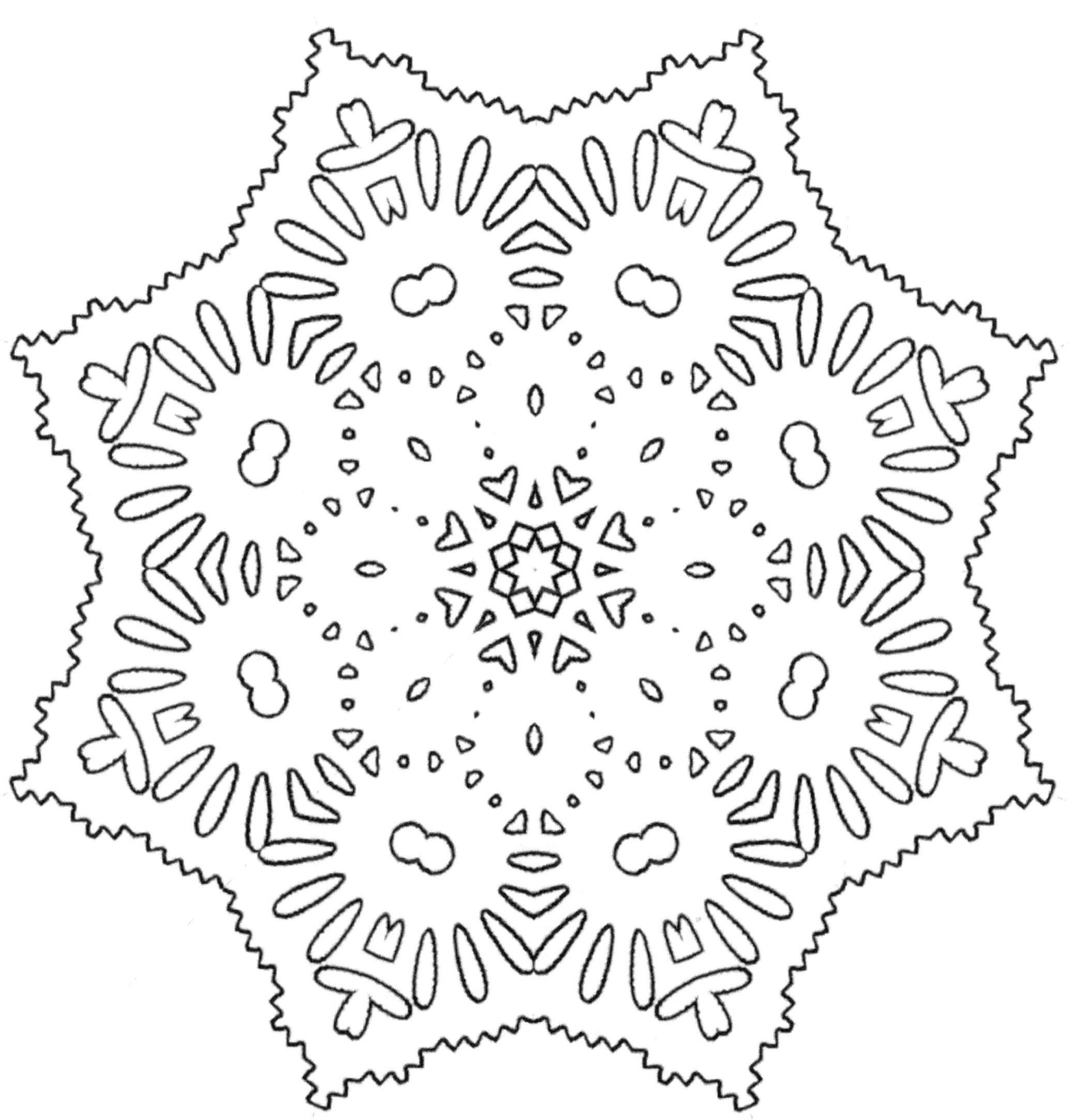

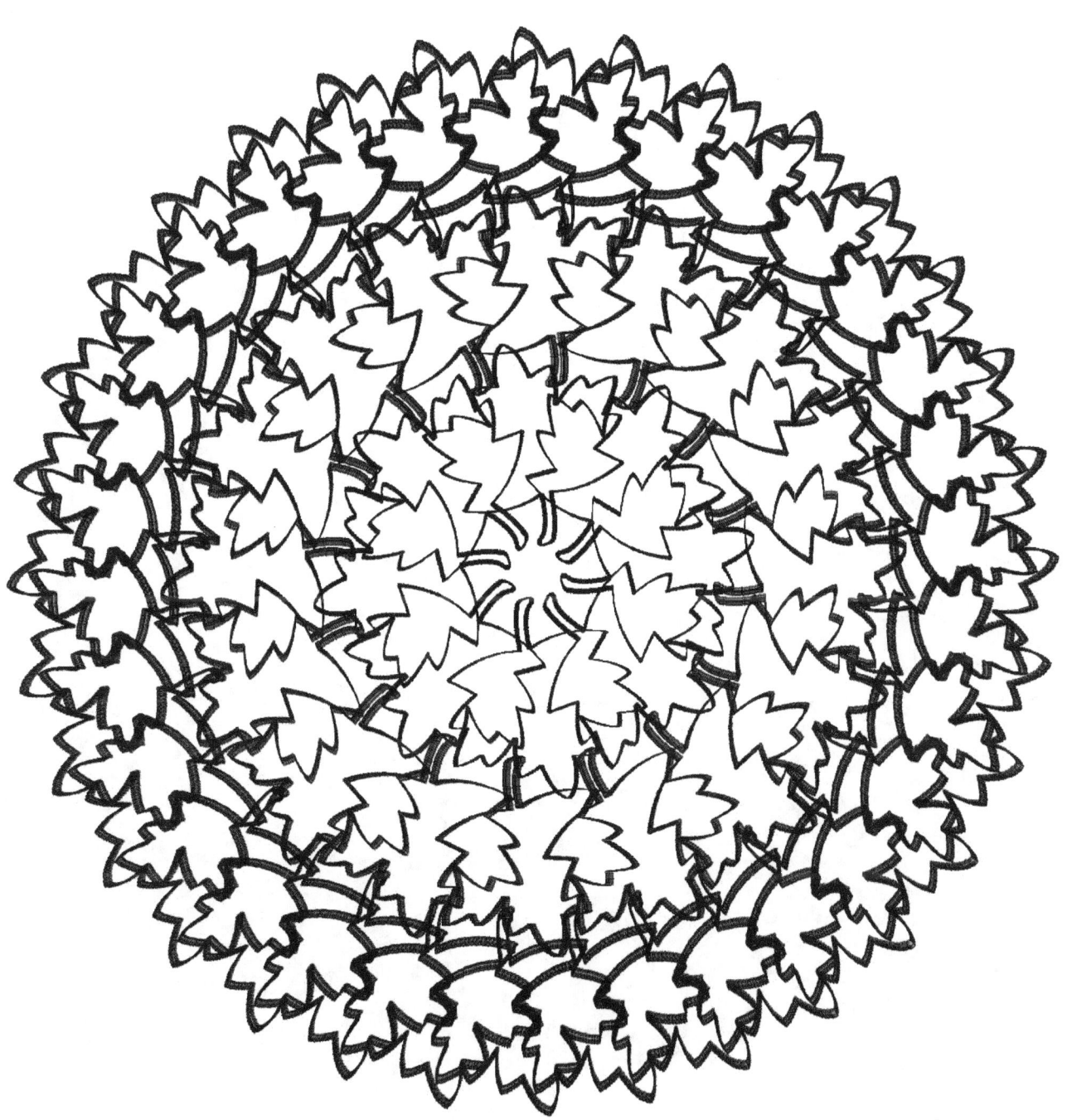

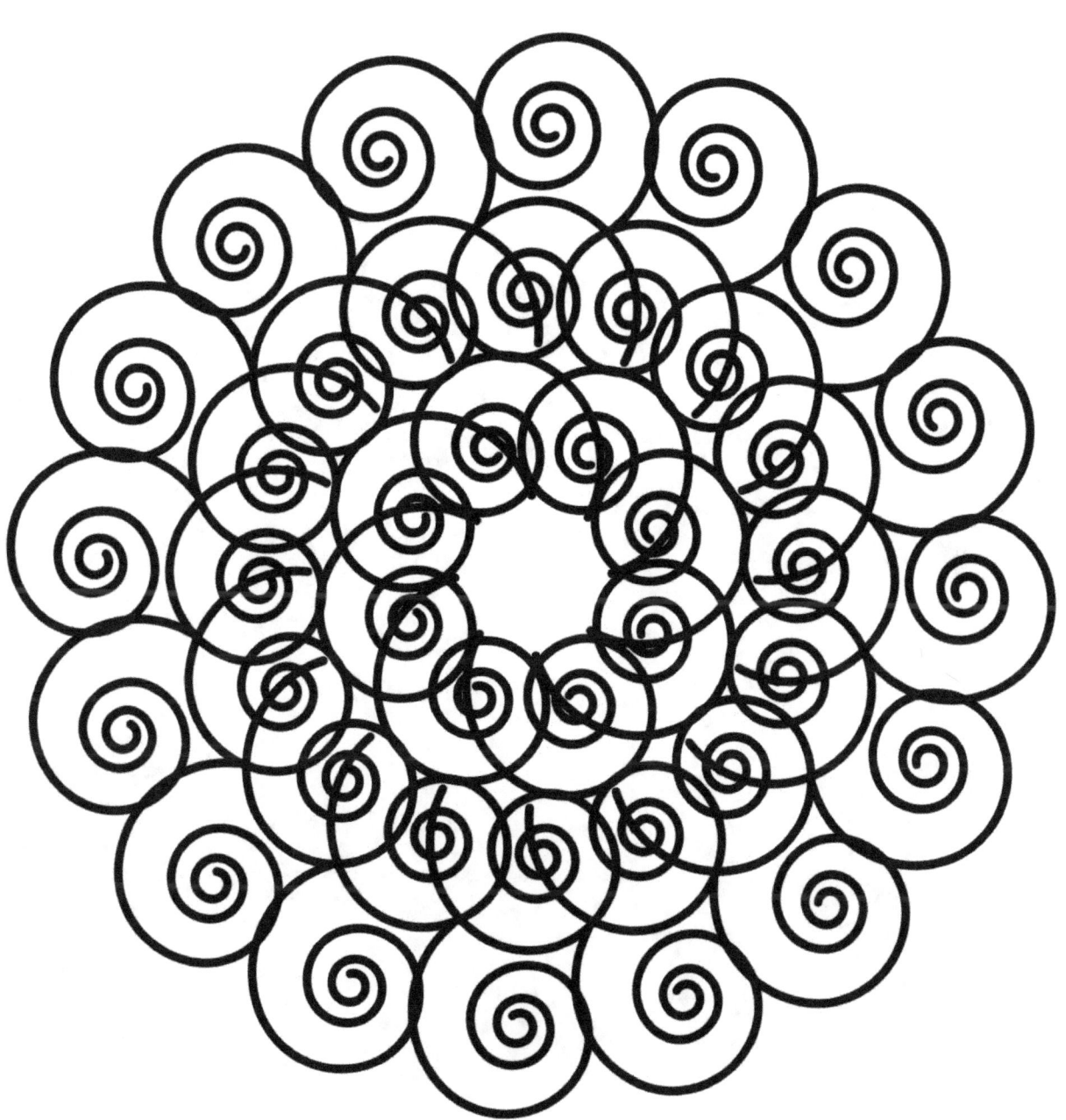

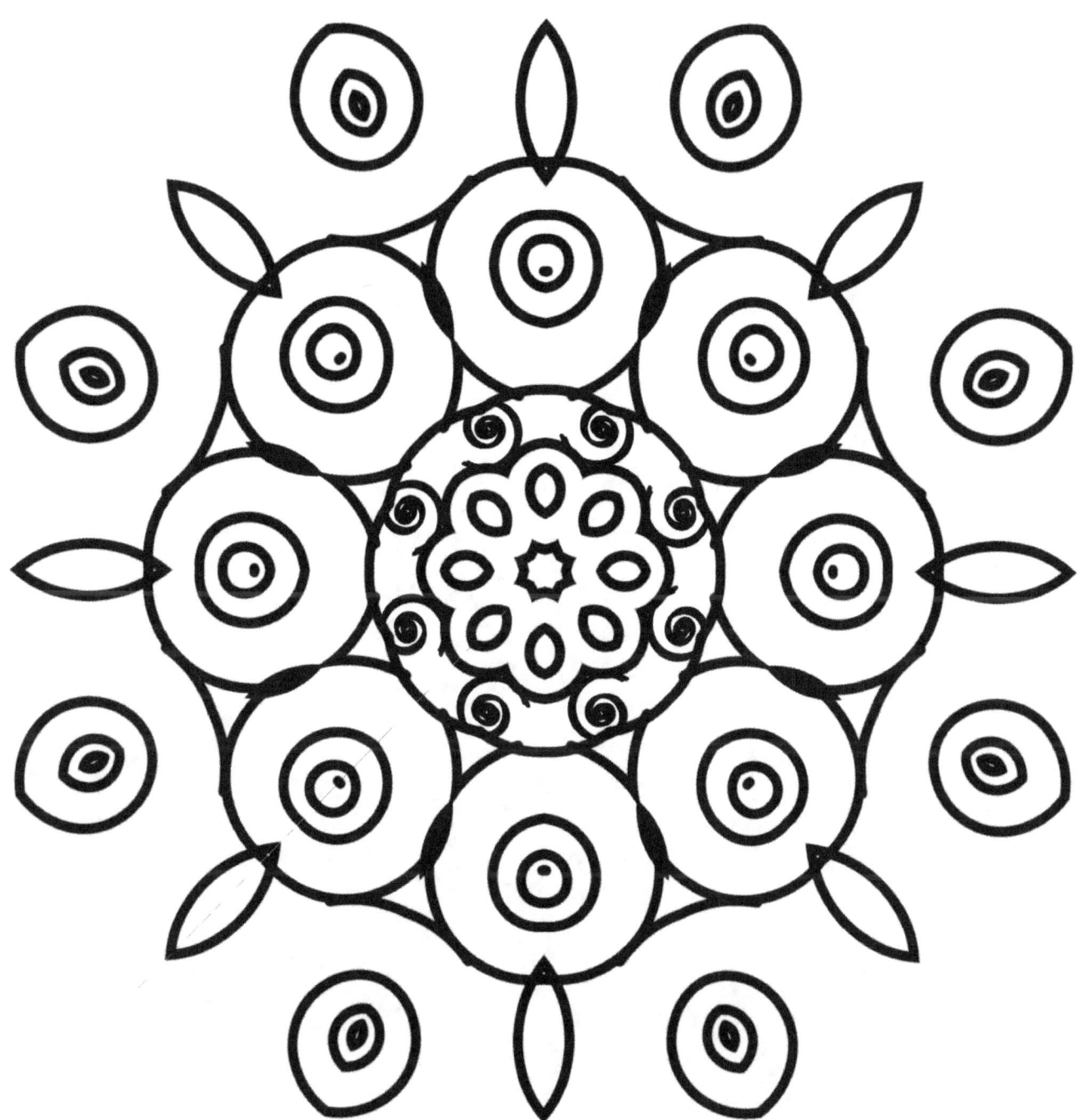

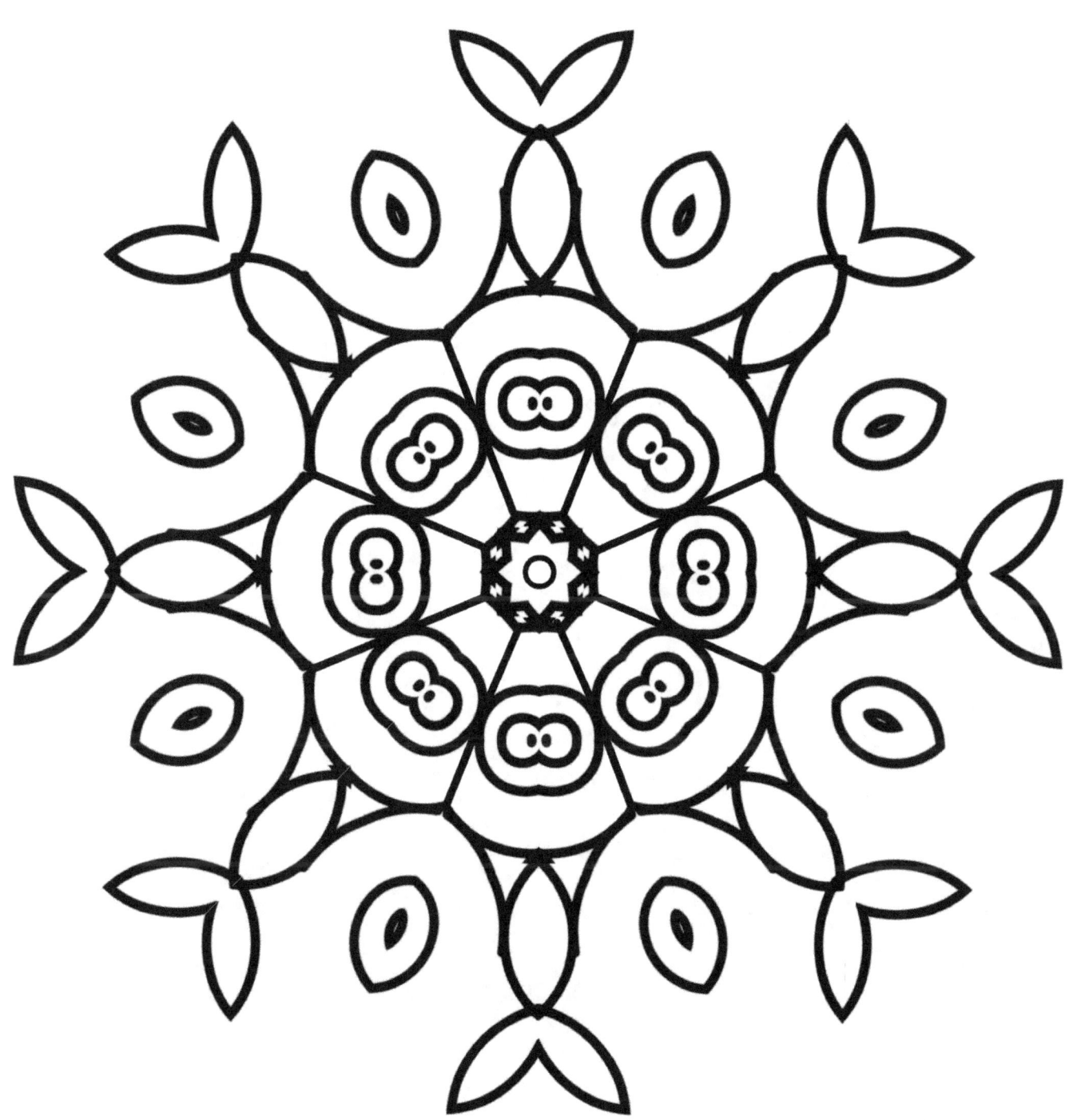

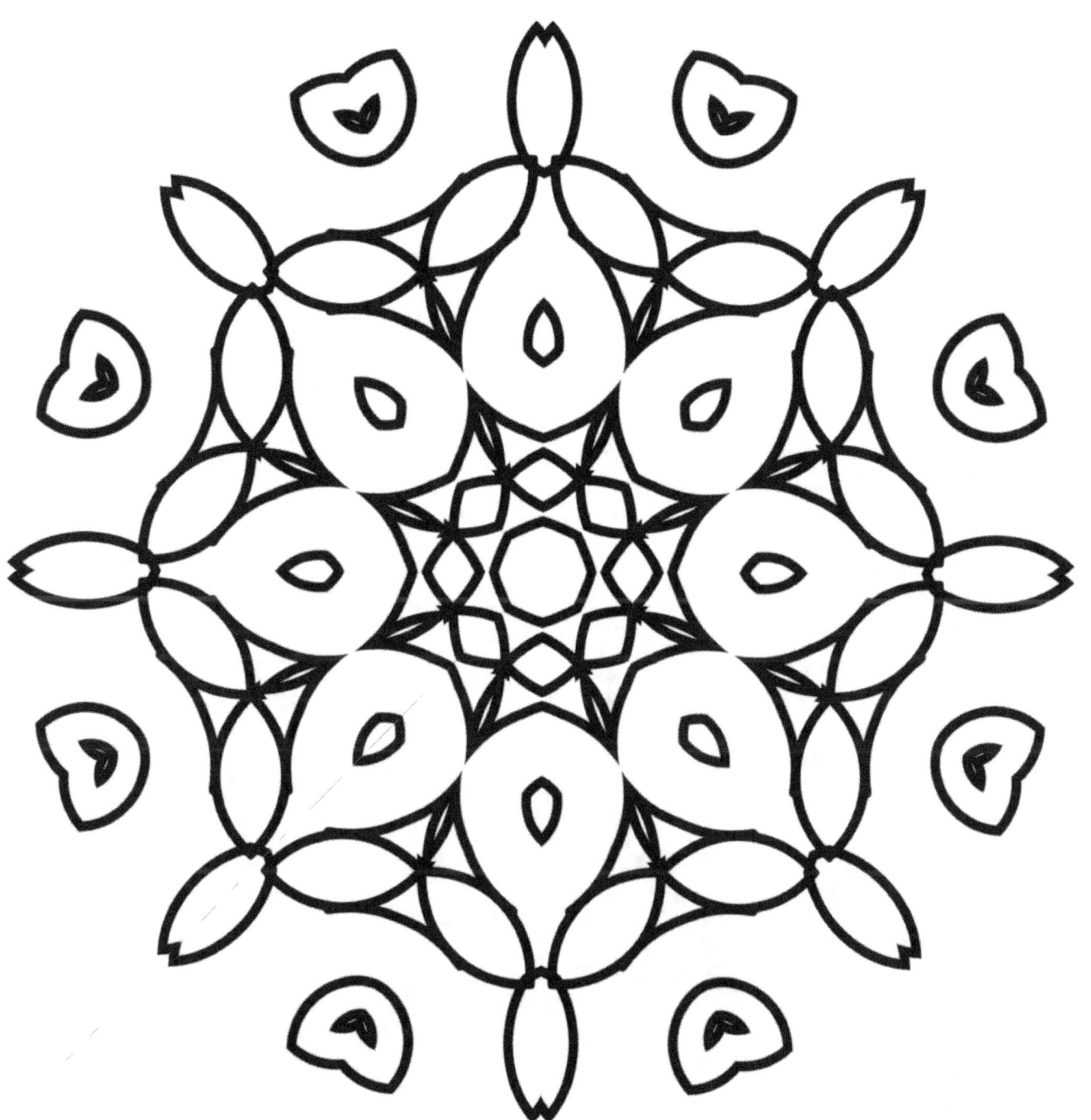

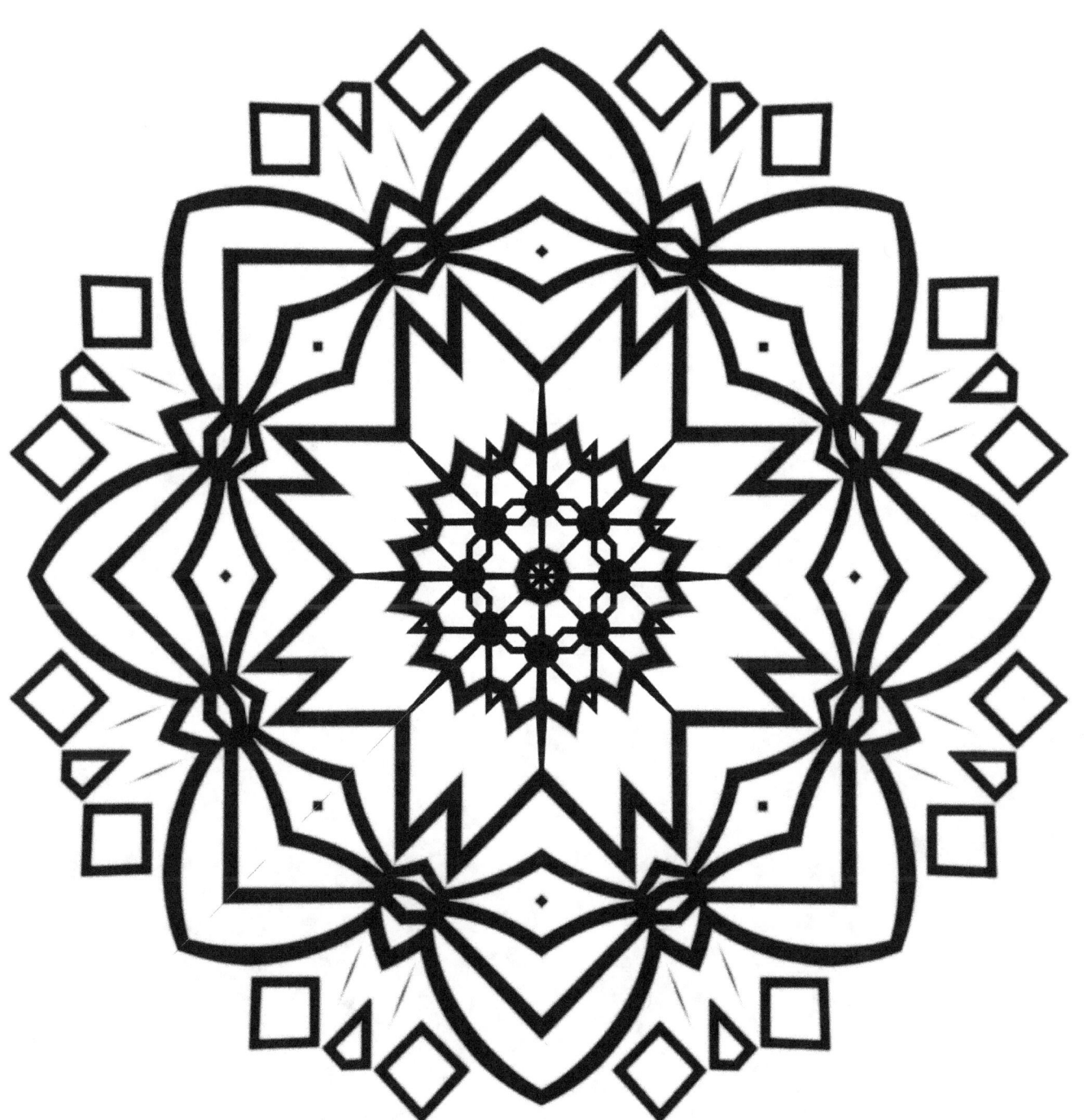

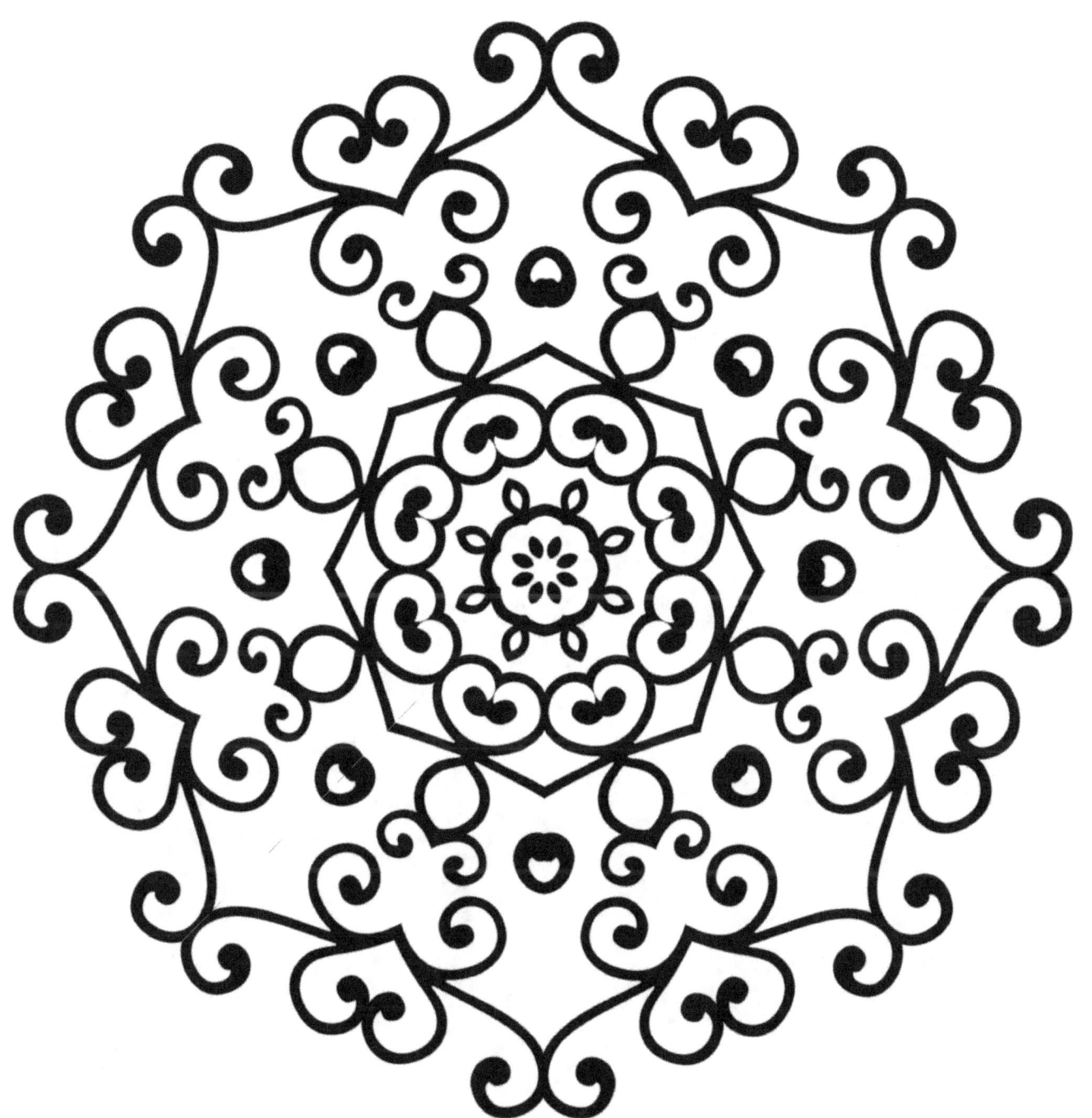

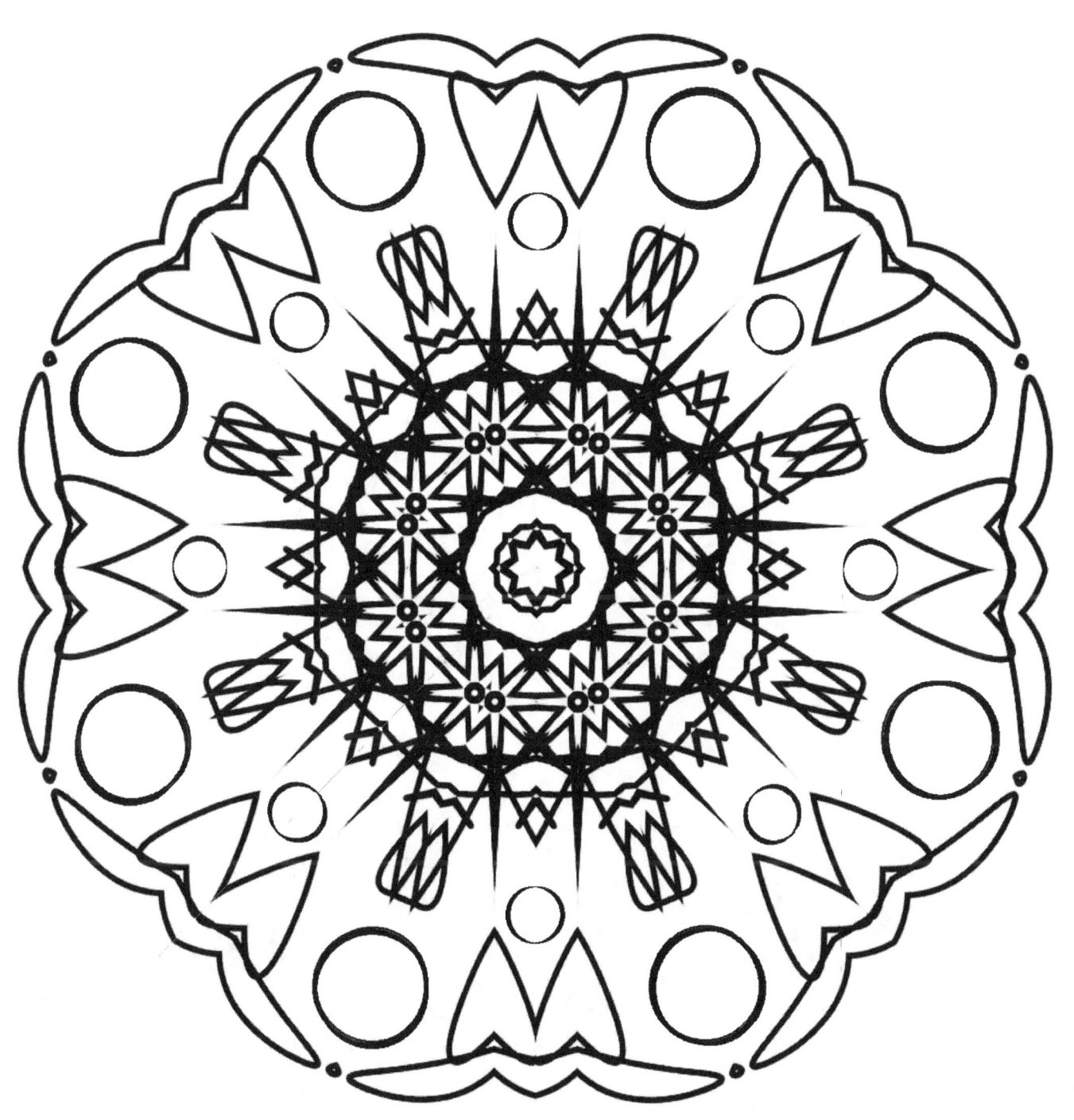

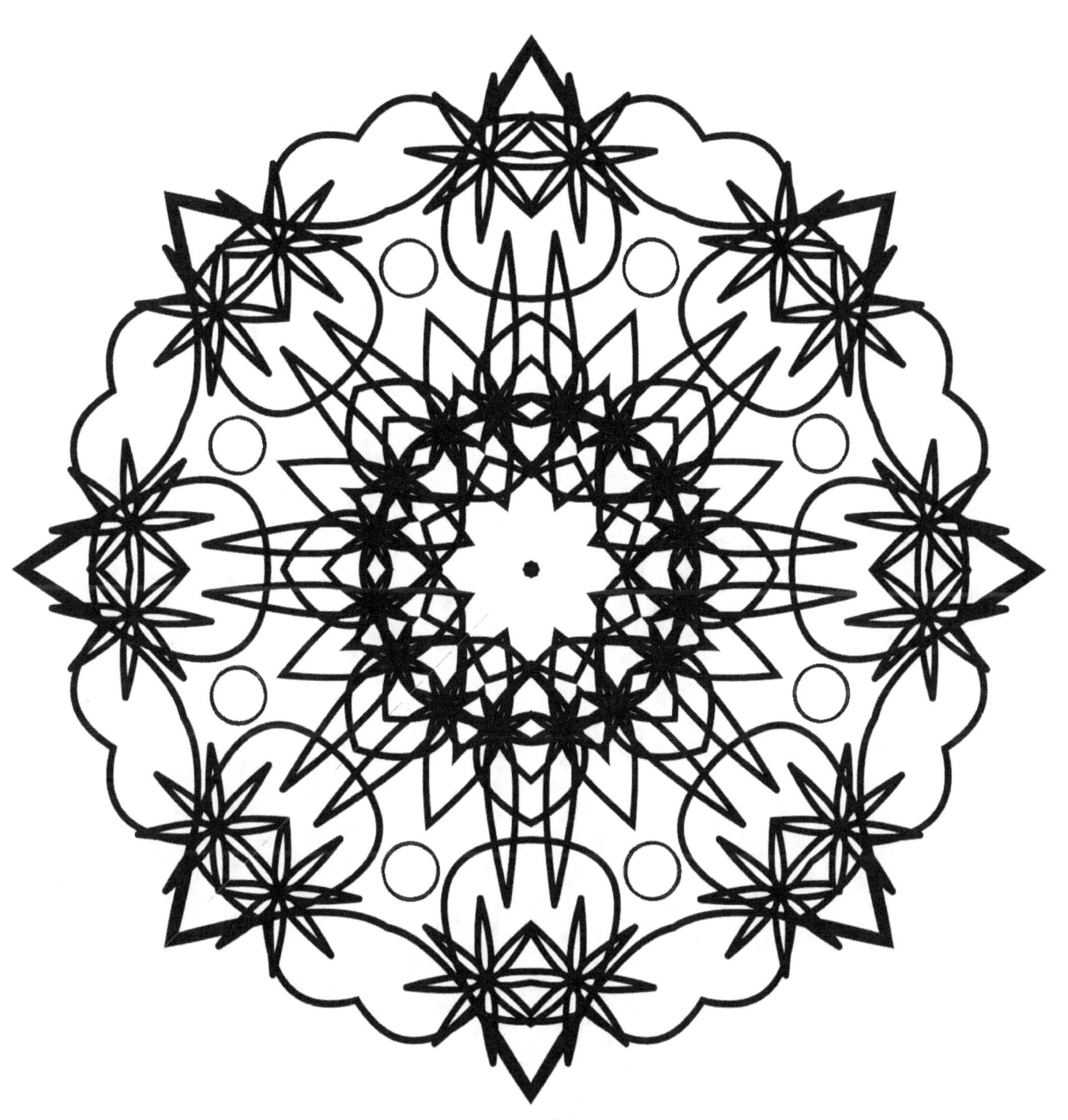

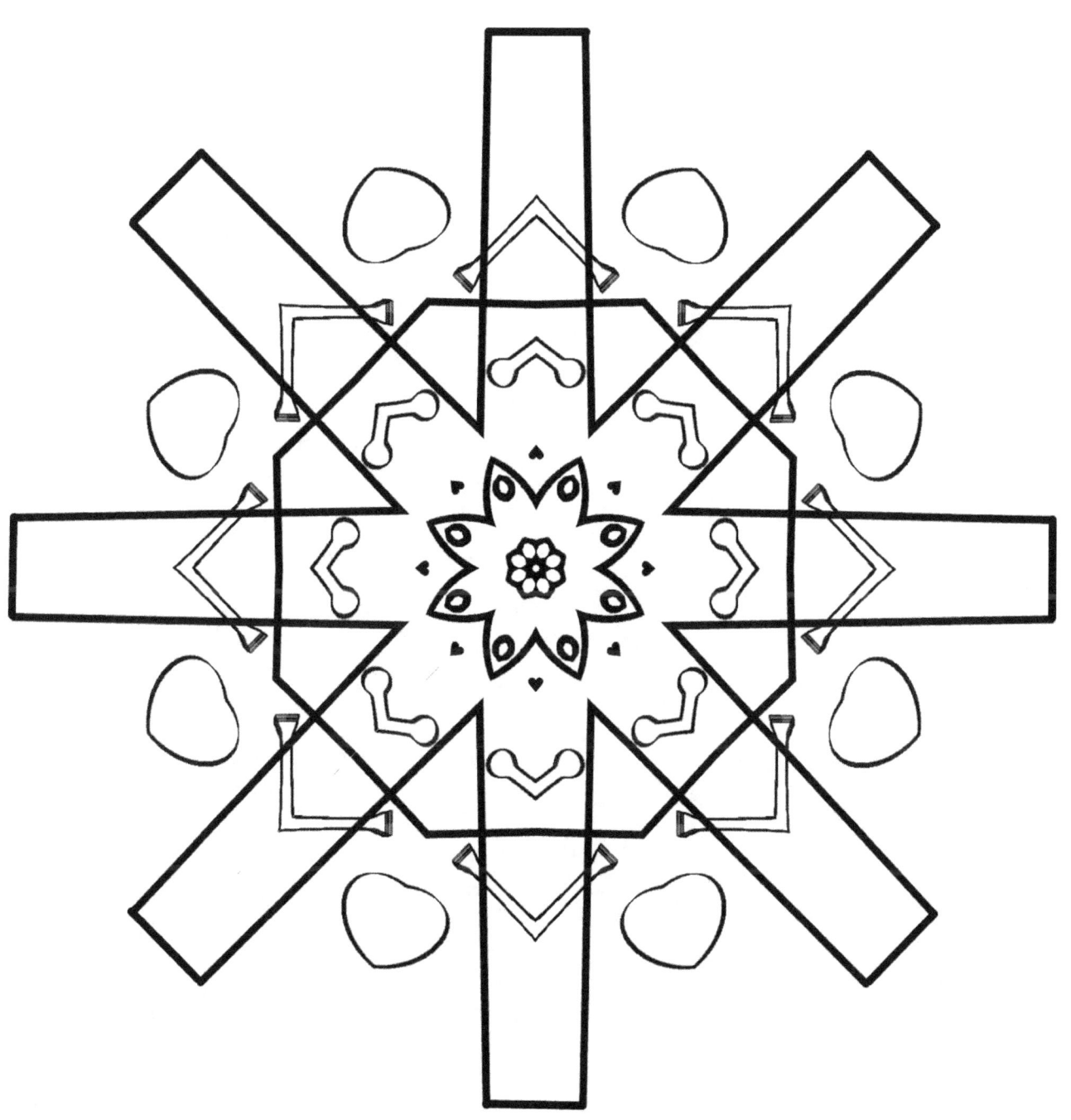

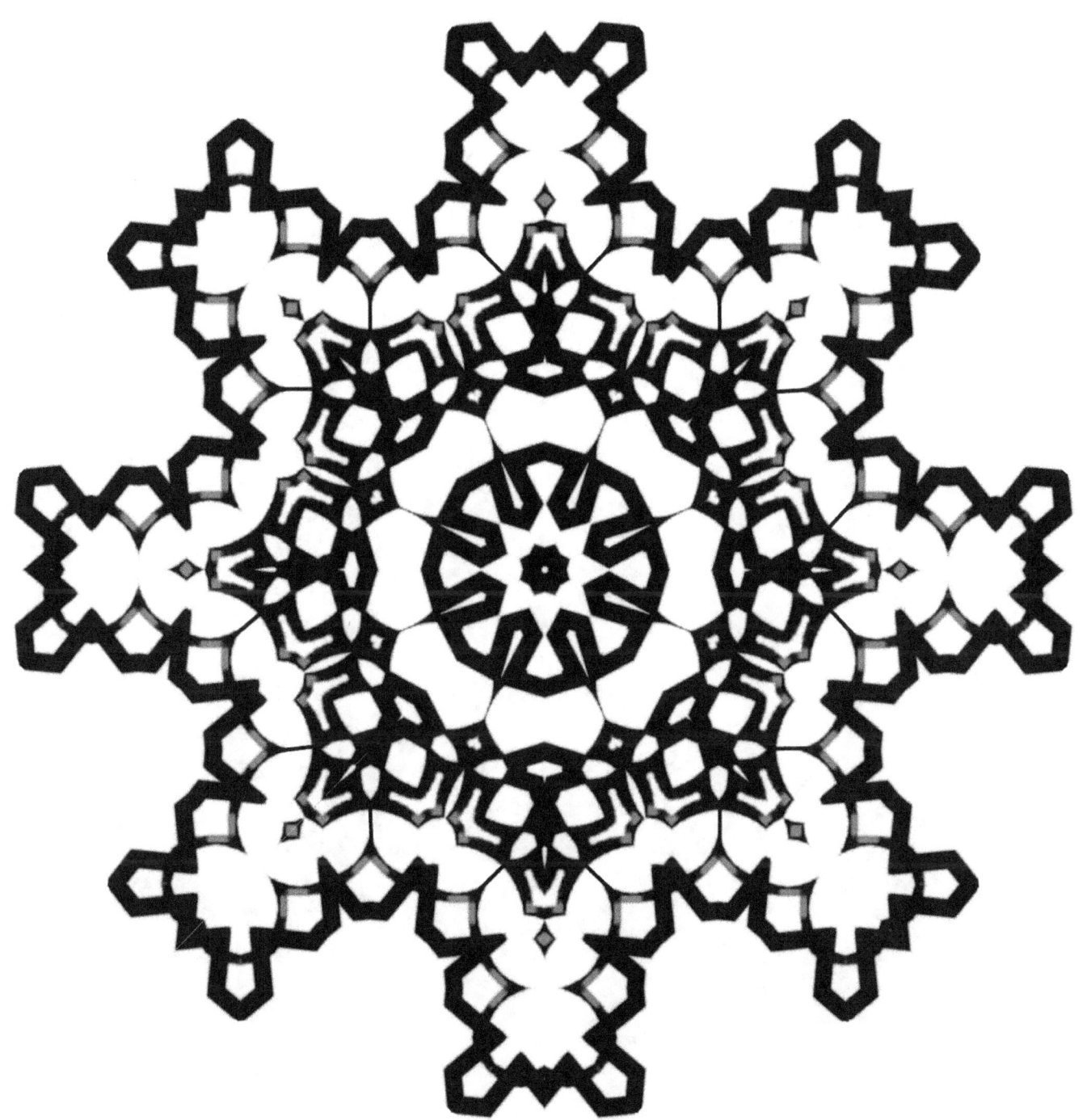

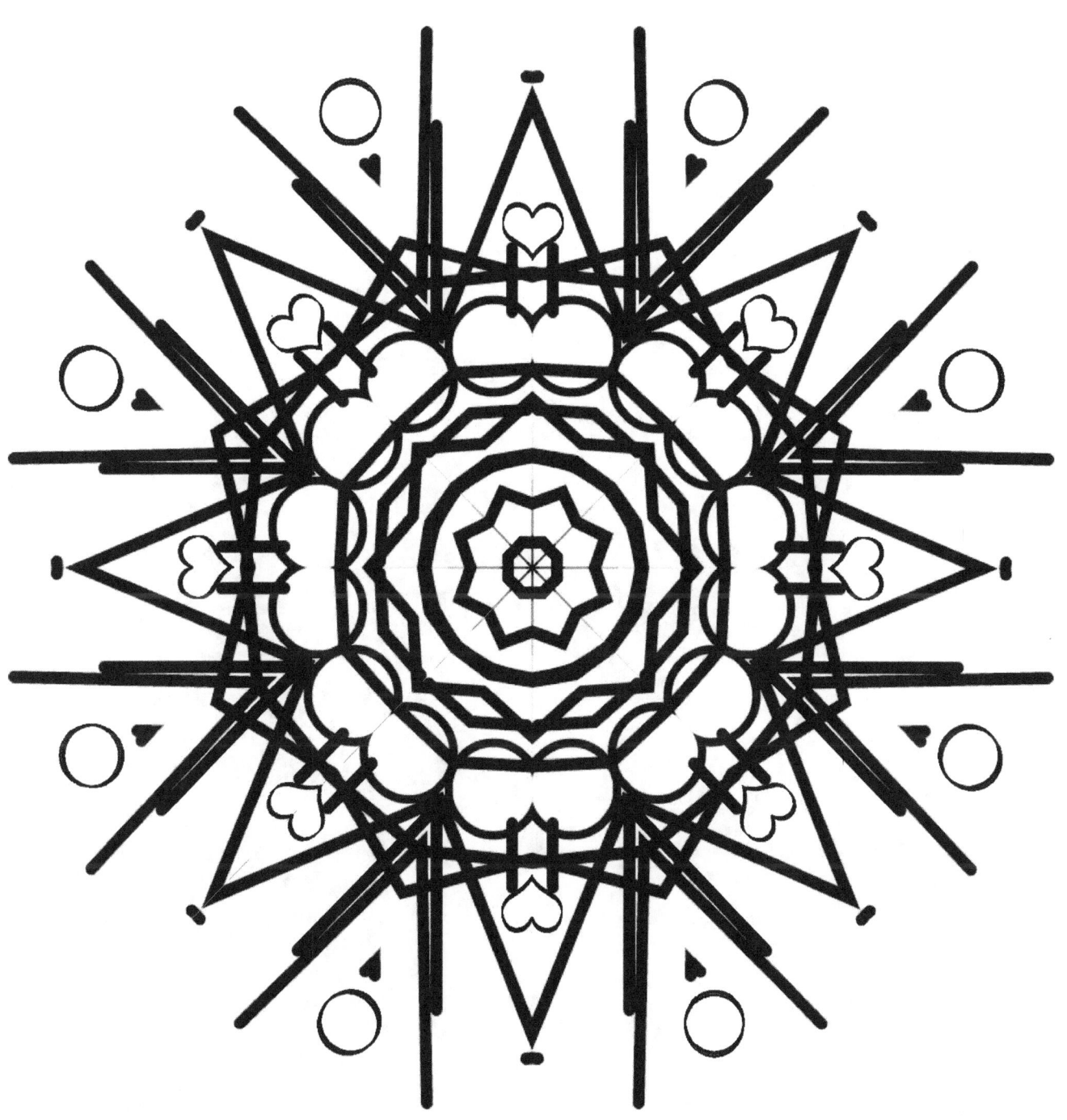

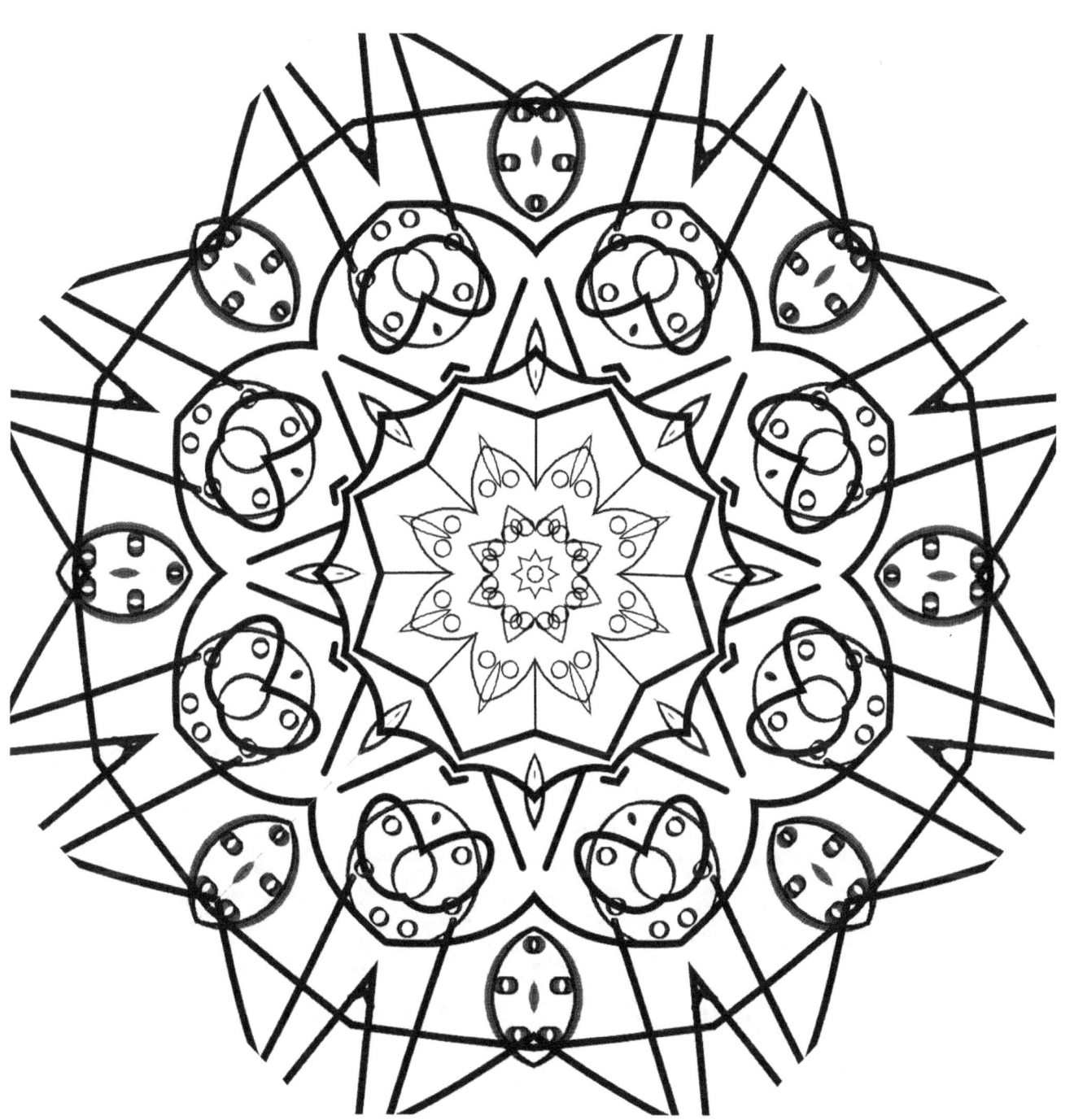

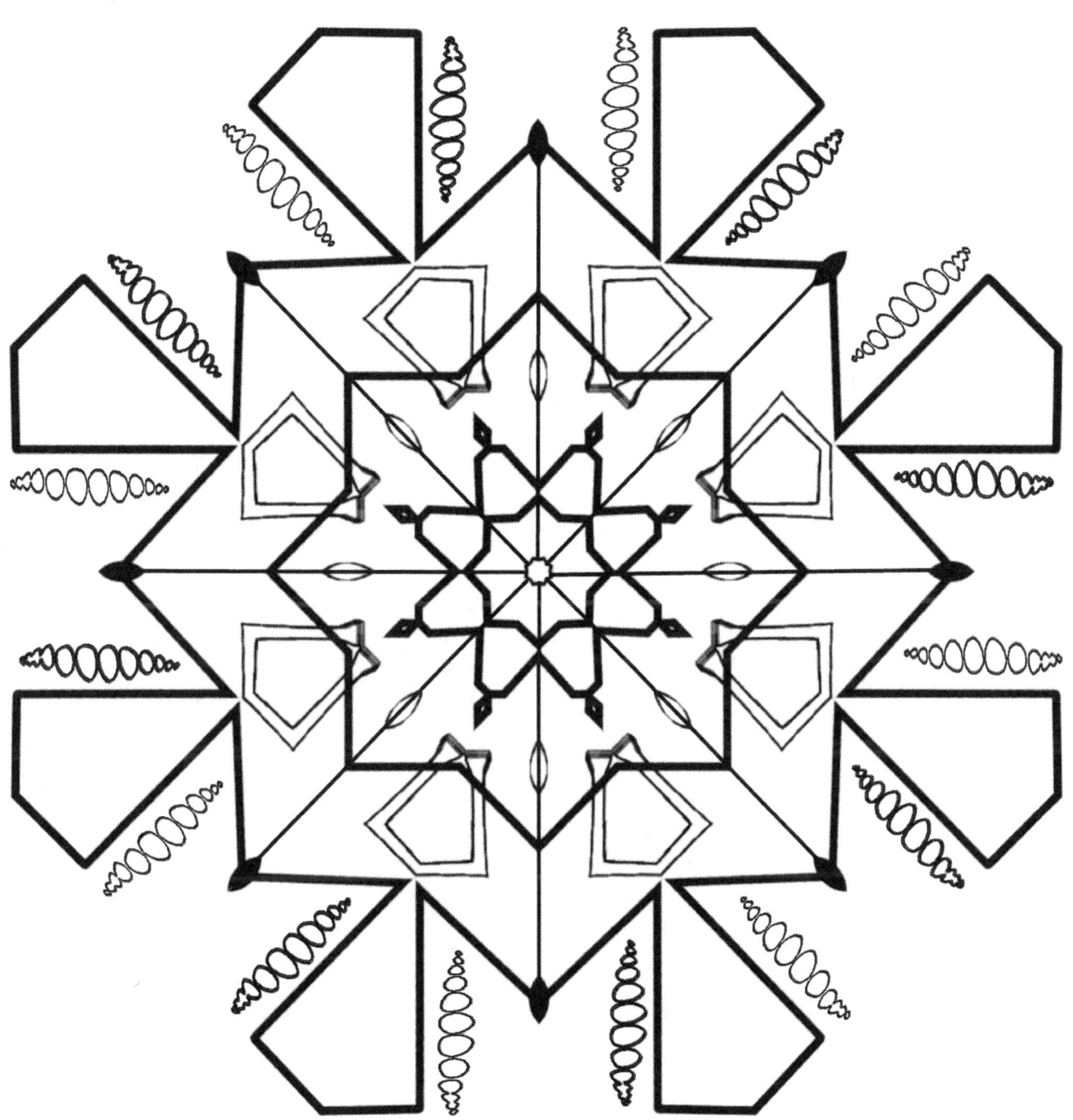

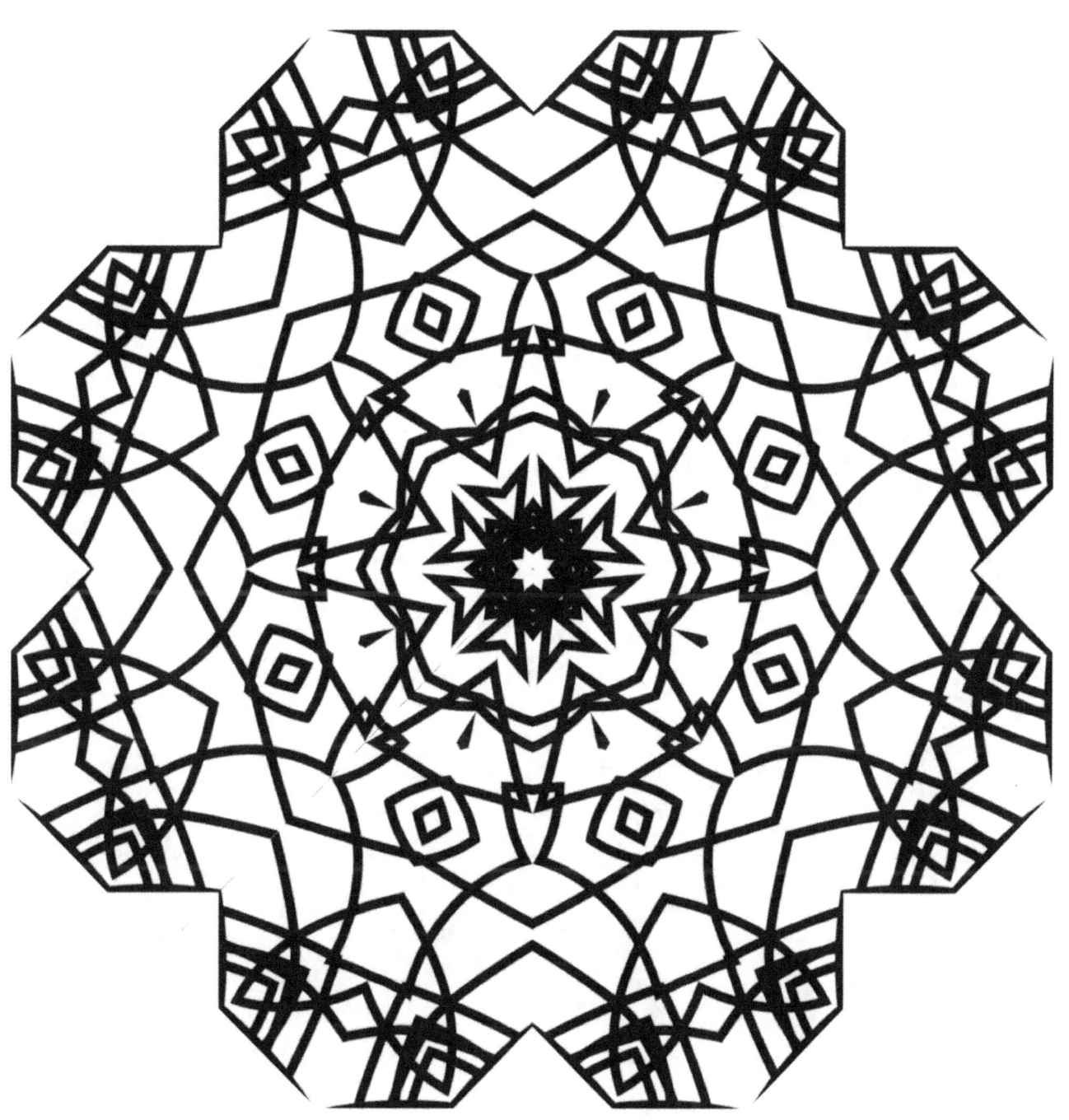

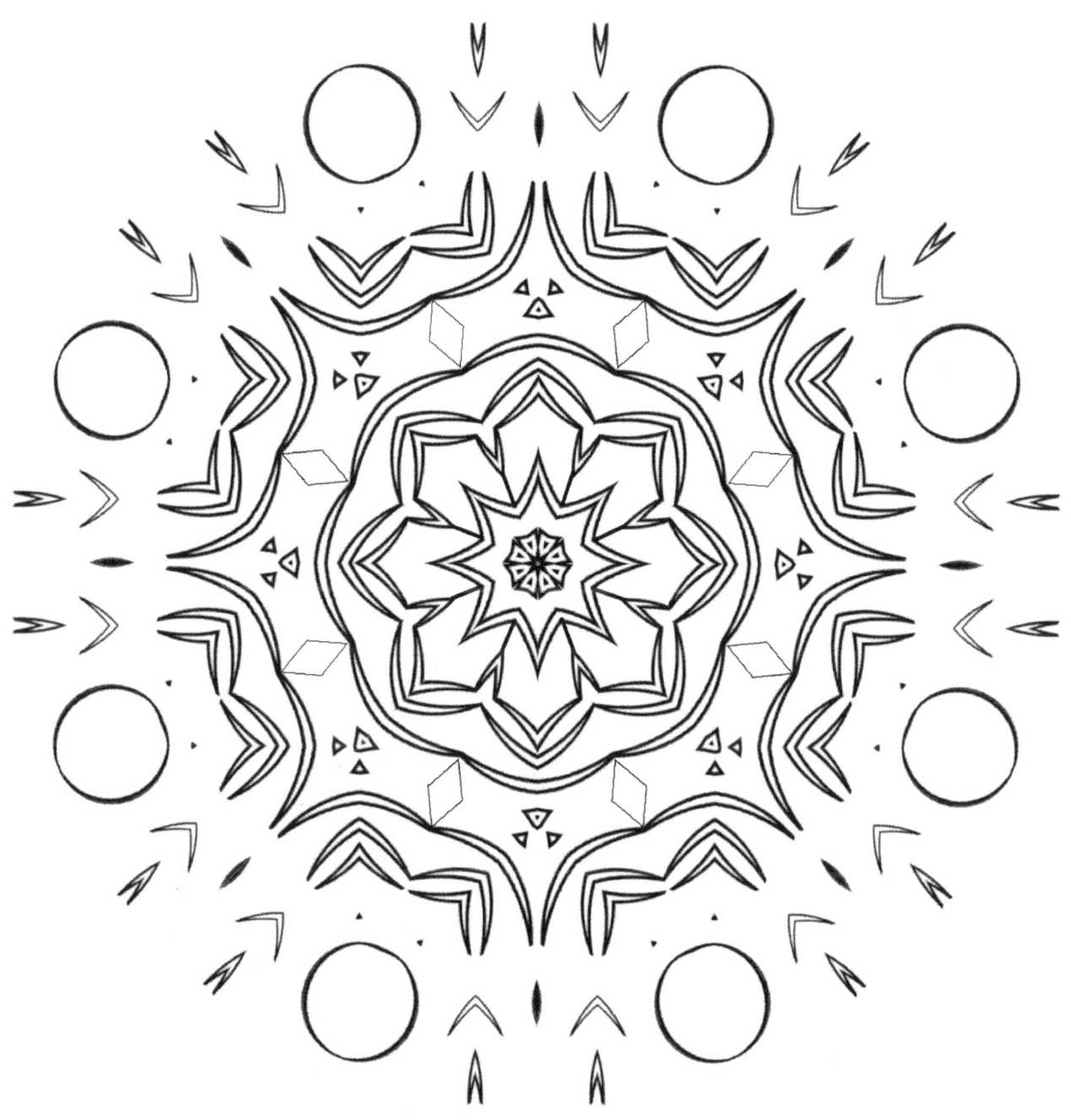

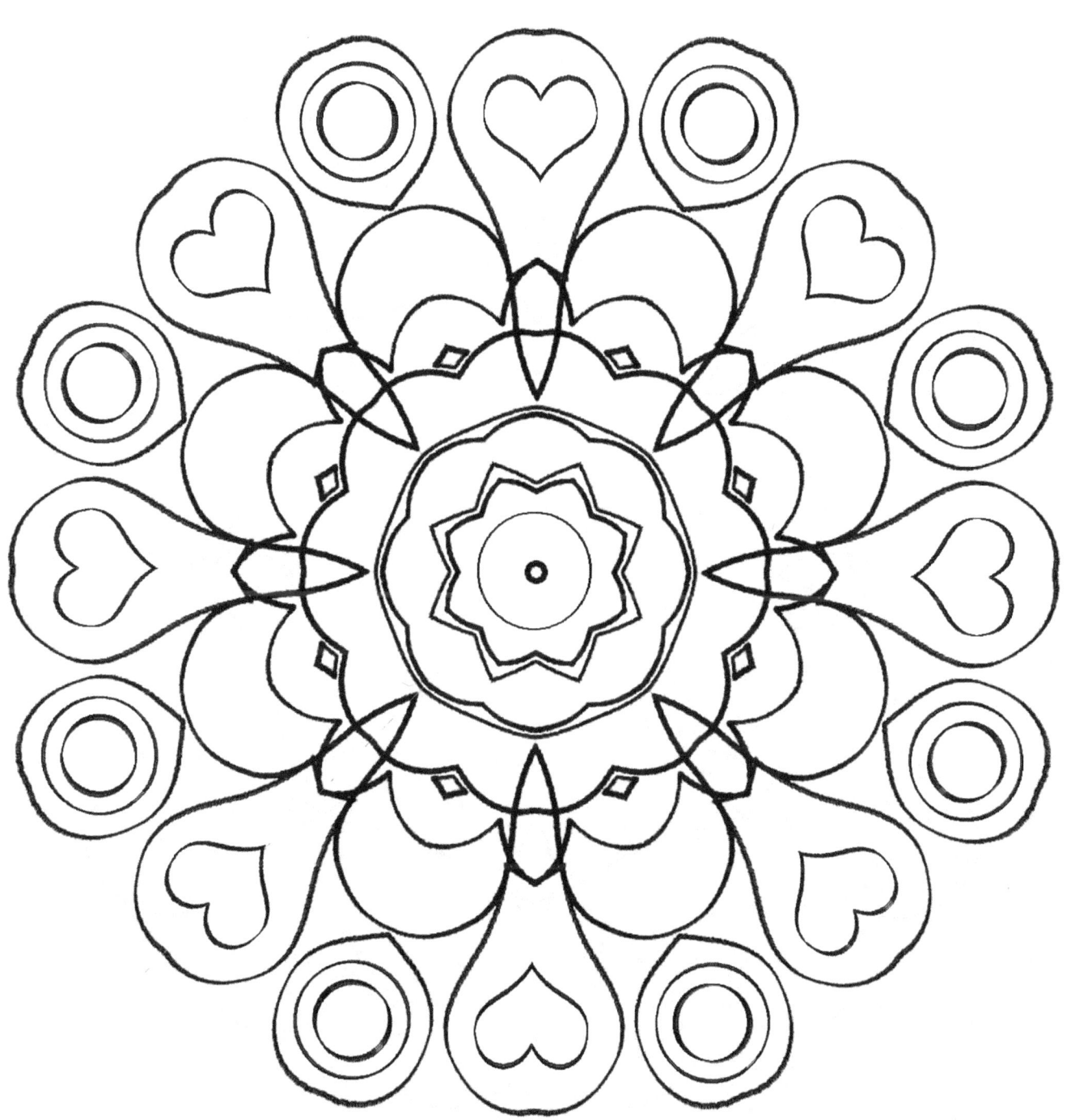

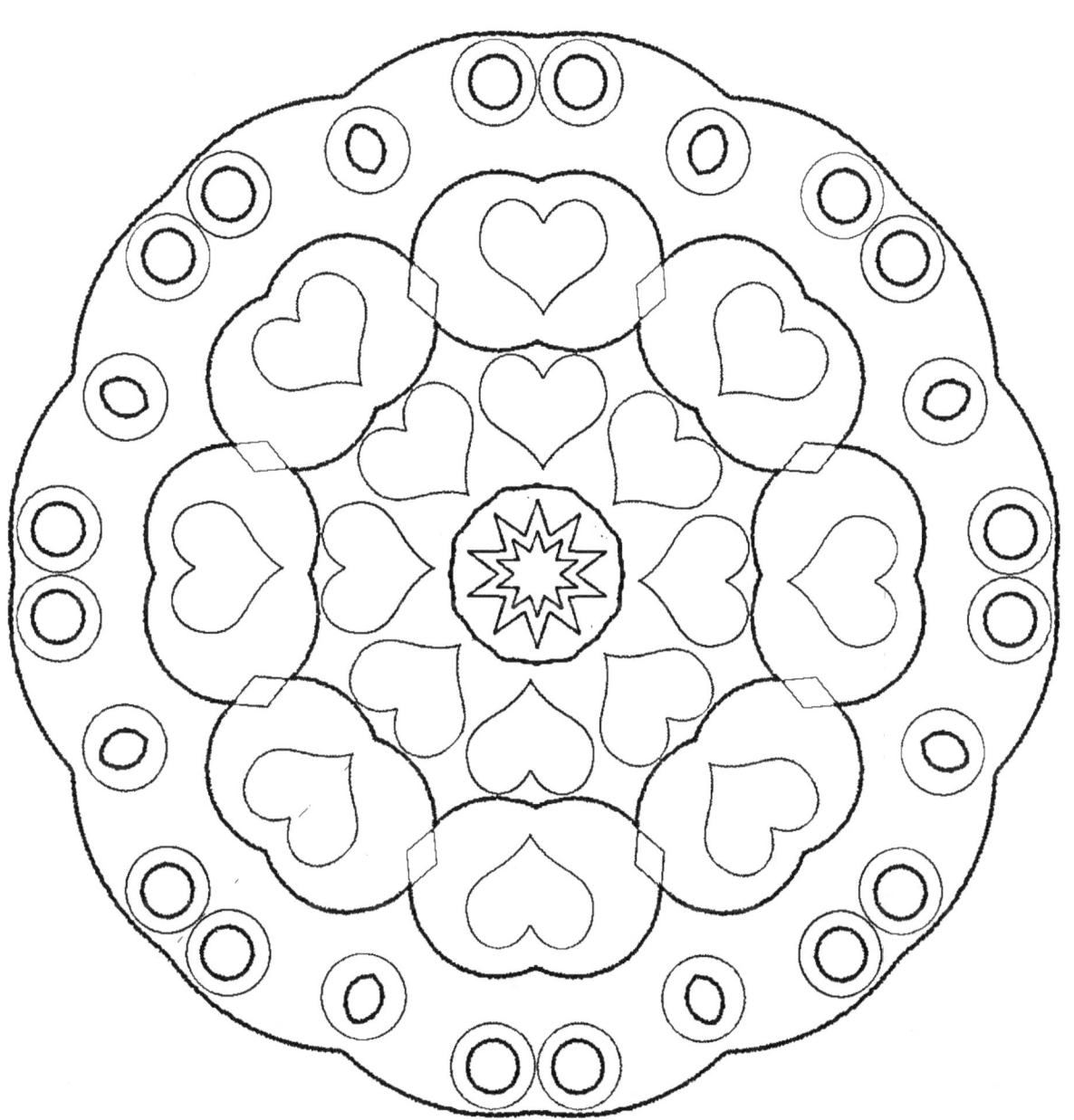

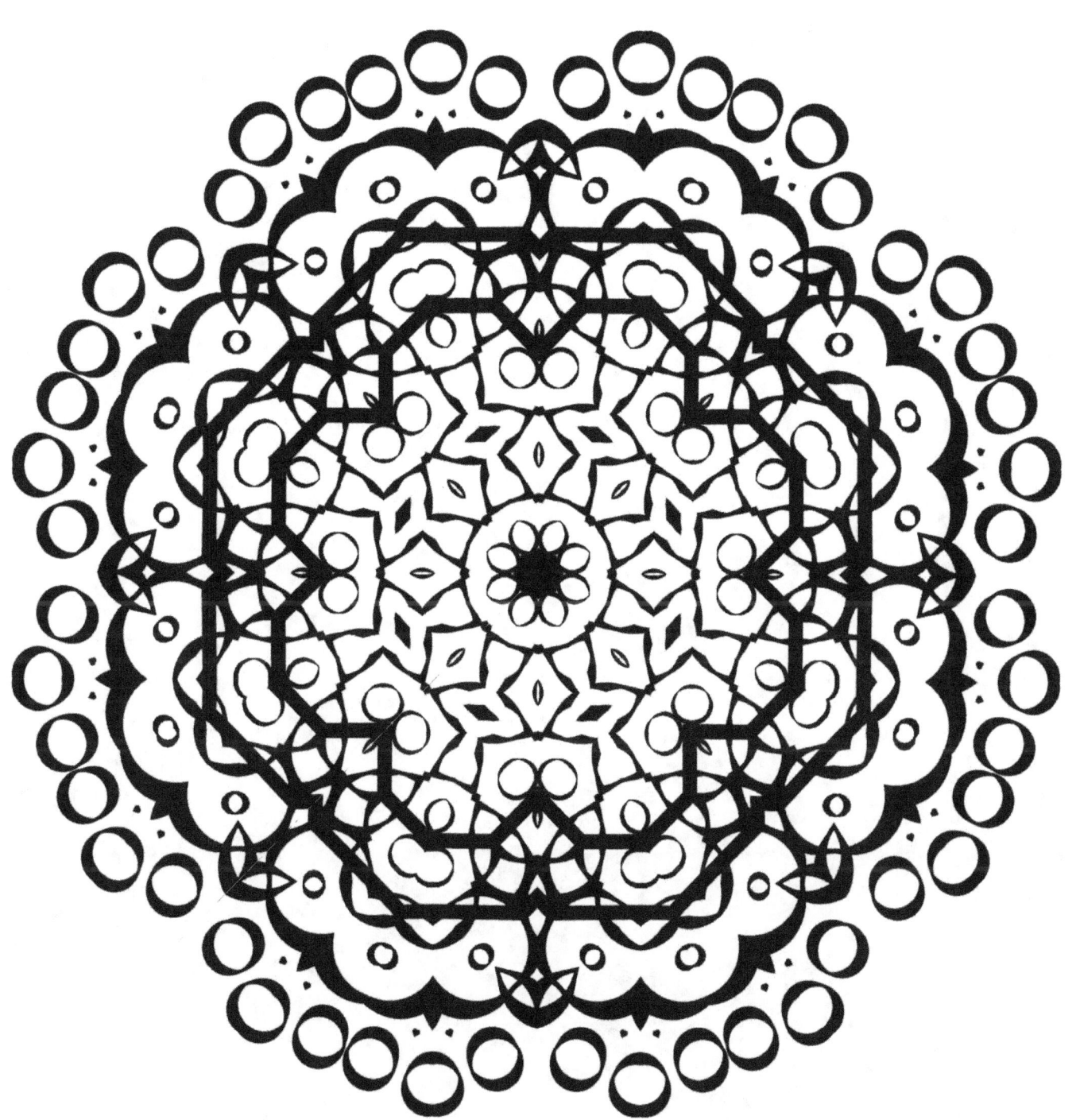

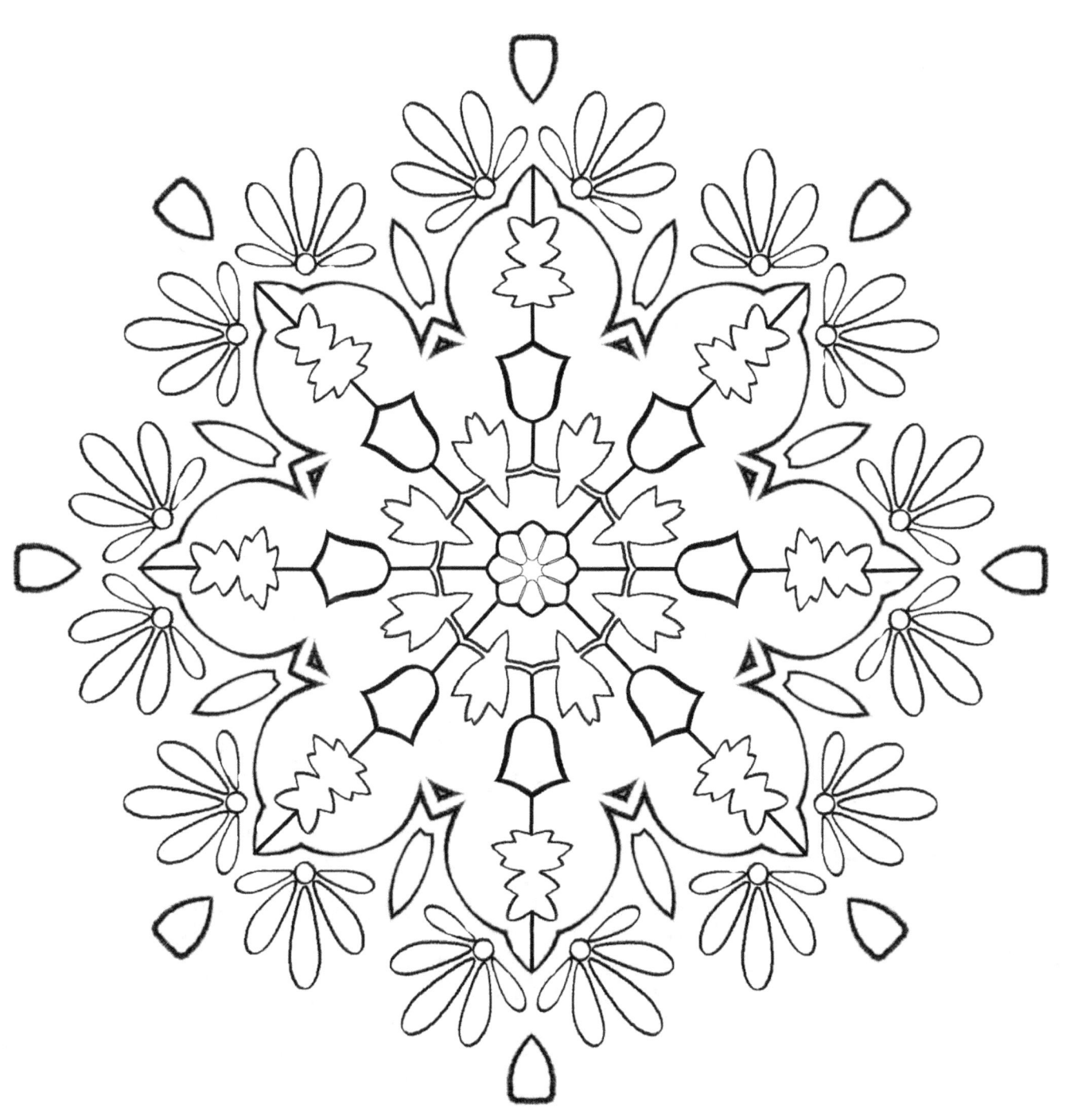

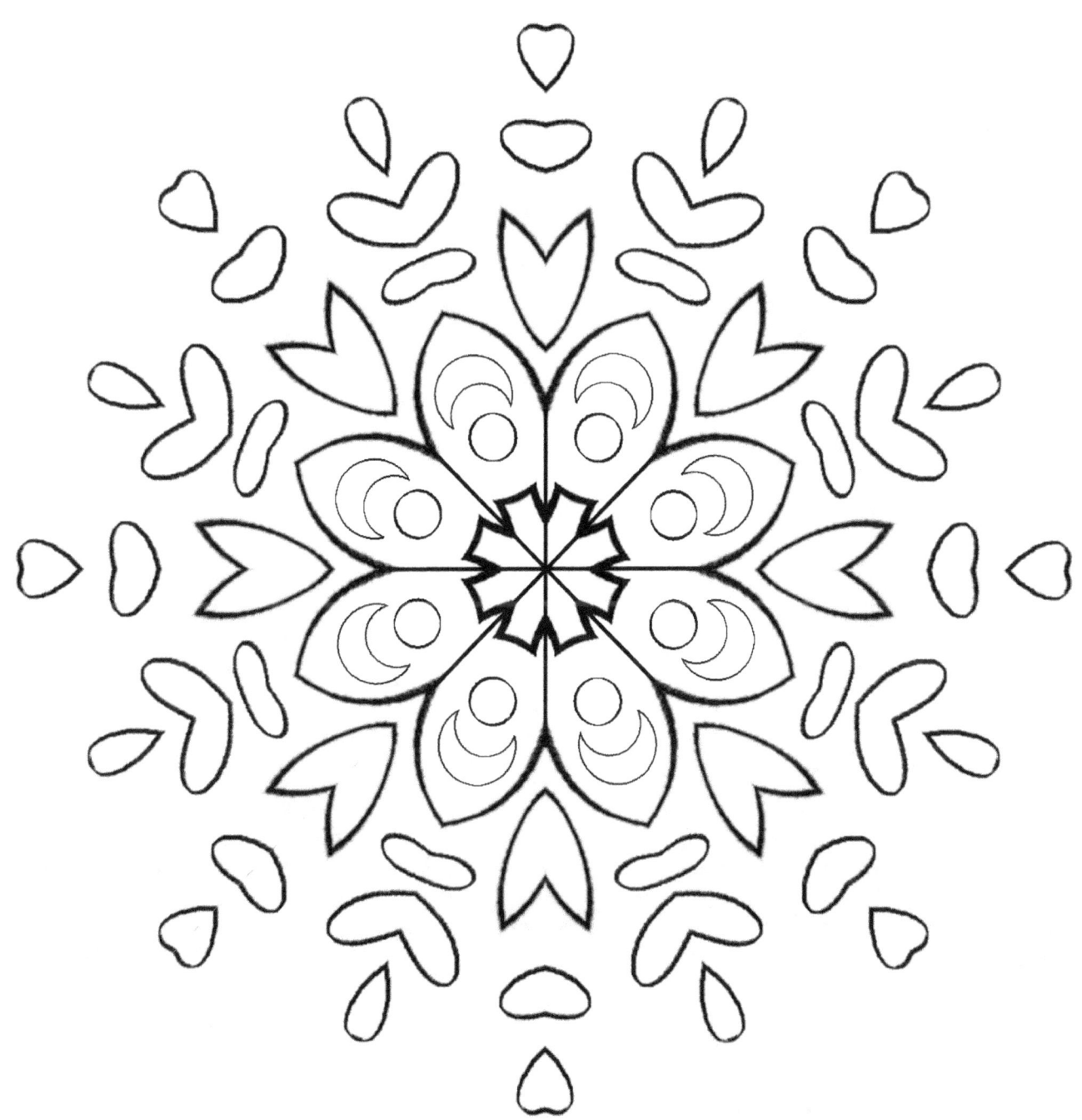

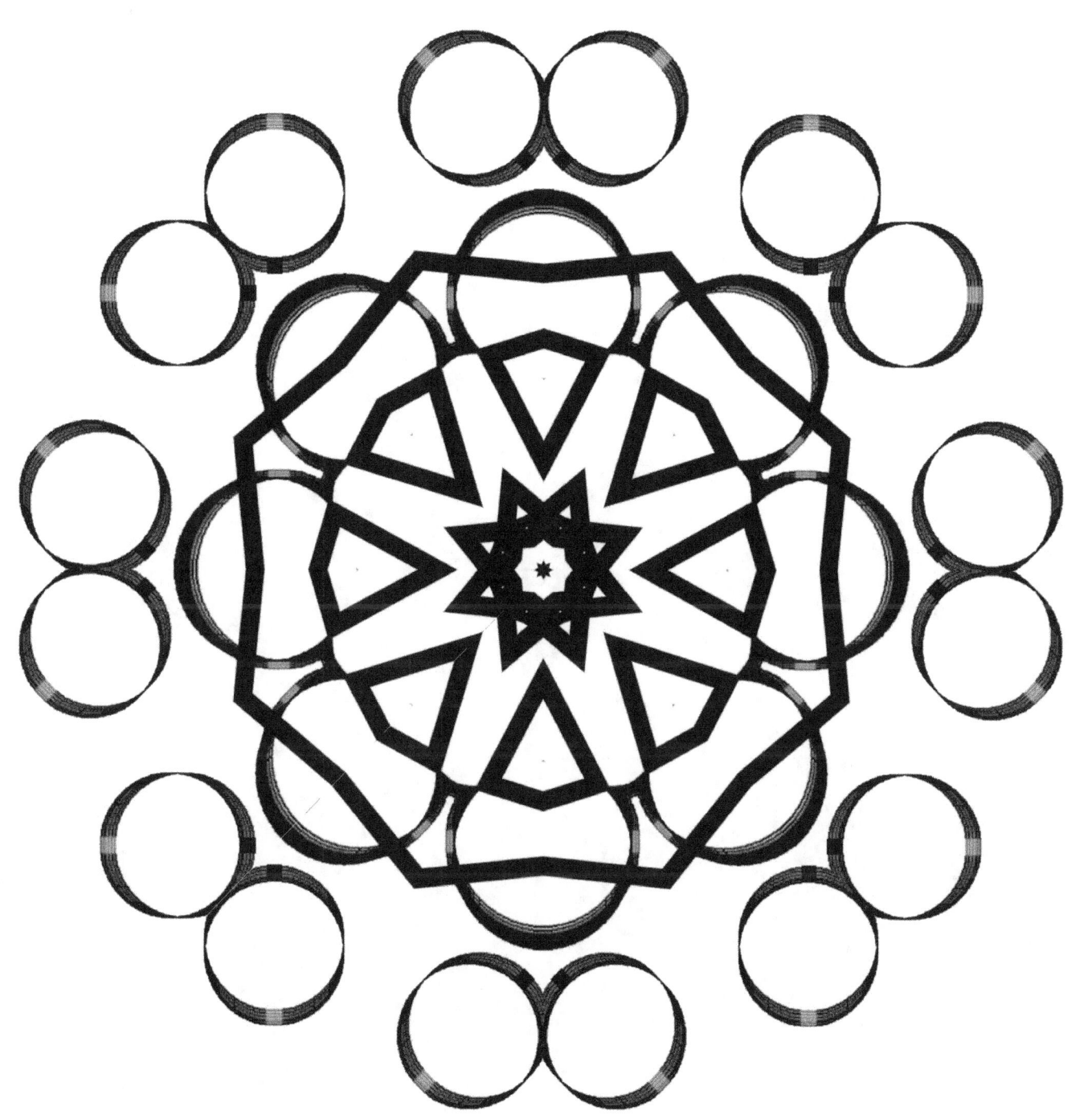

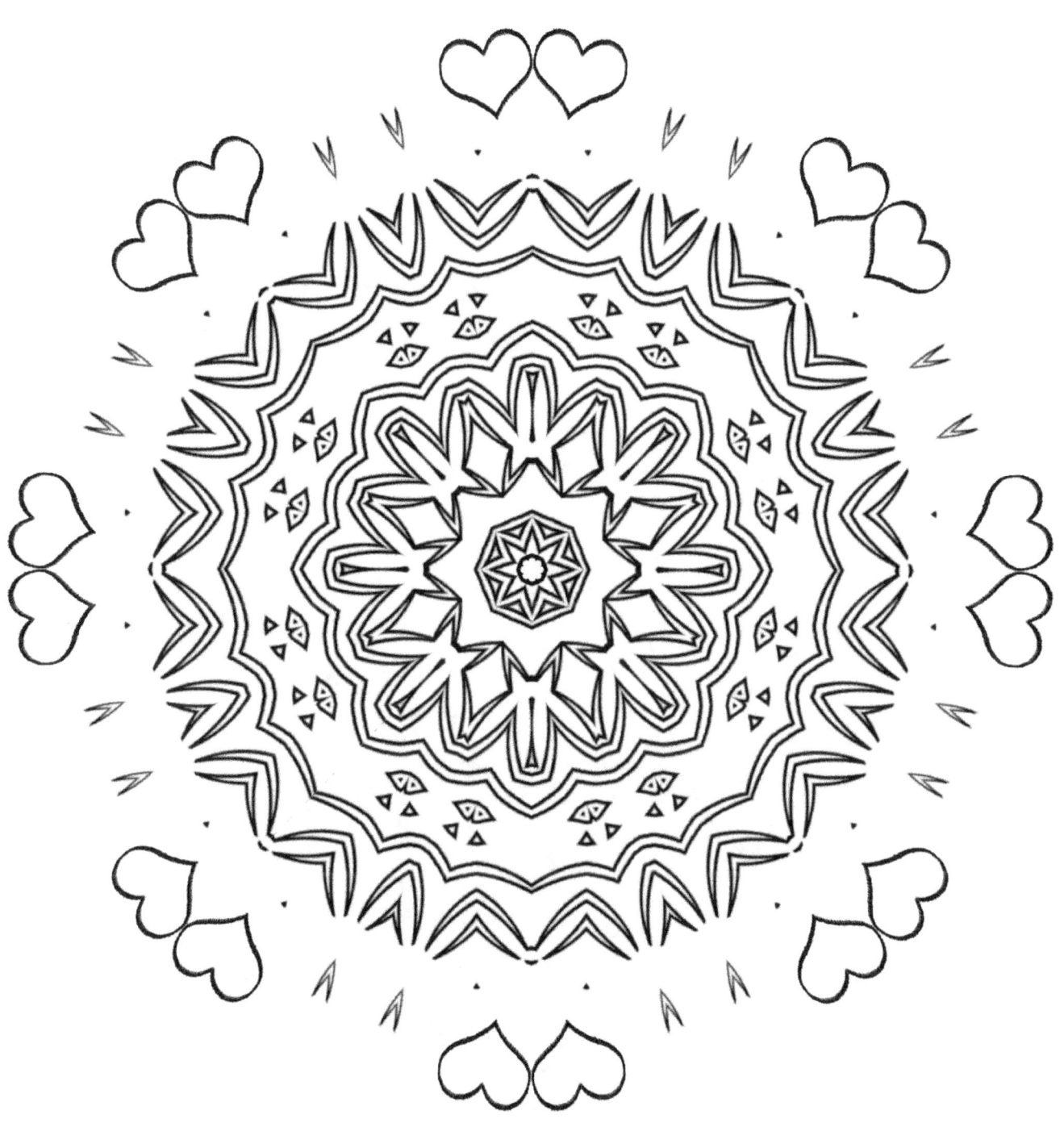

www.ingramcontent.com/pod-product-compliance
Lightning Source LLC
Chambersburg PA
CBHW081310170526
45166CB00011B/3474